CHOCOLATE
Canadian Living's best

BY

Elizabeth Baird

AND

The Food Writers of Canadian Living® Magazine
and The Canadian Living Test Kitchen

A MADISON PRESS BOOK
PRODUCED FOR
BALLANTINE BOOKS AND CANADIAN LIVING

Ballantine Books
A Division of
Random House of
Canada Limited
1265 Aerowood Drive
Mississauga, Ontario
Canada
L4W 1B9

Canadian Living
Telemedia
Communications Inc.
25 Sheppard Avenue West
Suite 100
North York, Ontario
Canada
M2N 6S7

Canadian Cataloguing in Publication Data

Baird, Elizabeth
Canadian Living's best chocolate

(Canadian living's best)
"A Madison Press Book".
Produced for Ballantine Books and Canadian Living.
ISBN 0-345-39851-3

1. Cookery (Chocolate). I. Title. II. Title: Chocolate. III. Series.

TX767.C5B33 1997   641.6'374   C97-931461-5

EDITORIAL DIRECTOR: Hugh Brewster
PROJECT EDITOR: Wanda Nowakowska
EDITORIAL ASSISTANCE: Beverley Renahan
PRODUCTION DIRECTOR: Susan Barrable
PRODUCTION COORDINATOR: Donna Chong
BOOK DESIGN AND LAYOUT: Gordon Sibley Design Inc.
COLOR SEPARATION: Colour Technologies
PRINTING AND BINDING: St. Joseph Printing Limited

CANADIAN LIVING ADVISORY BOARD: Elizabeth Baird, Bonnie Baker Cowan,
Anna Hobbs, Caren King

CANADIAN LIVING'S BEST CHOCOLATE
was produced by Madison Press Books
which is under the direction of Albert E. Cummings

Madison Press Books
40 Madison Avenue
Toronto, Ontario, Canada
M5R 2S1

Printed in Canada

Contents

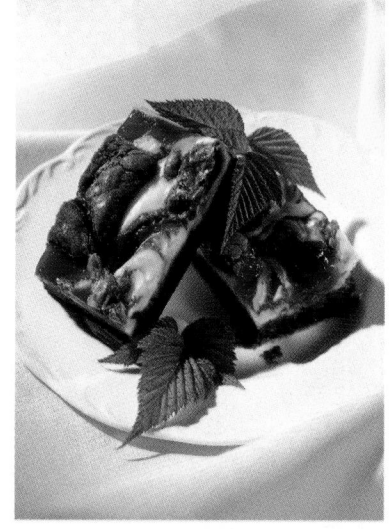

White Chocolate Lemon Tart (p. 34)

Introduction 5

Celebration Cakes 6

Pies and Tarts 34

Spoon Desserts 48

Cookies Galore 62

Sweets and Drinks 80

Credits and Index 90

Cream Cheese Raspberry Brownies (p. 73)

Introduction

There's no such thing as *liking* chocolate. It's a love affair from the first melting moment. As flavors go, chocolate is tops. It's more seductive than banana, gets people coming back for more encores than raspberry, surpasses caramel, outsells its bitter friend, coffee, and has hazelnuts, walnuts and pecans licked when it comes to popularity.

And why? For one thing, chocolate melts at body temperature, making it a delight to nibble and encouraging that "just one more" kind of feeling. And, while chocolate is more in demand than the flavors above (just check what gets eaten first on a tray of cookies or is chosen most often on the dessert menu), it's also a great mixer — with the very same fruit, nuts, caramel and coffee, to more than double the applause and the pleasure.

Then, there's just chocolate itself, offering so many shades and flavor variations — milk, white and sweet chocolate for the beginner chocolate lover; semisweet and, even better, bittersweet for the chocolate connoisseur. And while it's true that chocolate, *xocolatl*, started out as an Aztec drink in pre-Columbian Mexico, and hot chocolate still meets coffee and tea head-on in the hot-drink category, there's so much more to chocolate than a steaming marshmallow-topped mug. Cookies, squares, ice cream, sorbets, puddings, pies, tarts, cakes, gooey icings, thick sauces, truffles, fudge, crunchy chocolate bark...and the list goes on.

You'll find them all, and much more, in this definitive collection of over 100 chocolate recipes no chocolate lover will want to be without. *Canadian Living's Best Chocolate* — need we say more?

Elizabeth Baird

Chocolate Hazelnut Dacquoise
(recipe, p. 8)

Celebration Cakes

A cake is a cake is a celebration. Birthdays, weddings, showers, graduations, anniversaries — a cake in all its finery marks these milestones in life. And what's the favorite flavor? Chocolate, hands-down winner for any special occasion.

Three-Layer Chocolate Fudge Cake ▶

Everyone needs a really good recipe for a dense, rich, chocolaty chocolate layer cake. And here it is, in anticipation of birthdays, anniversaries and other special occasions. For the icing on the cake, choose a sophisticated Chocolate Buttercream (recipe follows) or our luscious Best-Ever Chocolate Icing (recipe, p. 24) which is featured on the cover.

Per serving (with Chocolate Buttercream): about
- 670 calories
- 45 g fat
- good source of iron
- 7 g protein
- 67 g carbohydrate

Chocolate Buttercream per 1/4 cup (50 mL): about
- 275 calories
- 24 g fat
- 2 g protein
- 17 g carbohydrate

1 cup	unsweetened cocoa powder	250 mL
1 cup	unsalted butter, softened	250 mL
2 cups	granulated sugar	500 mL
3	eggs	3
2 tsp	vanilla	10 mL
2 oz	semisweet chocolate, melted and cooled	60 g
3 cups	sifted cake-and-pastry flour	750 mL
2 tsp	baking powder	10 mL
1 tsp	baking soda	5 mL
Pinch	salt	Pinch
	Chocolate Buttercream (recipe follows)	

● Grease three 9-inch (1.5 L) round cake pans. Line bottoms with waxed paper; set aside.

● In bowl, whisk cocoa powder with 1-1/2 cups (375 mL) boiling water until smooth. Let cool to room temperature.

● In large bowl, beat butter until fluffy; gradually beat in sugar until light and fluffy. Beat in eggs, one at a time, beating well after each addition. Beat in vanilla. On low speed, beat in melted chocolate.

● In separate bowl, stir together flour, baking powder, baking soda and salt. Using wooden spoon, stir into chocolate mixture alternately with cocoa mixture, making three additions of flour mixture and two of cocoa mixture. Divide among prepared pans.

● Bake in center of 350°F (180°C) oven for 30 to 40 minutes or until cake tester inserted in center comes out clean. Let cool in pans on racks for 15 minutes. Remove from pans; let cool completely on racks. *(Cakes can be wrapped in plastic wrap and stored at room temperature for up to 1 day or over-wrapped in foil and frozen in rigid airtight container for up to 1 month.)*

● Peel paper from one of the cake layers; place on plate. Spread top with 1 cup (250 mL) of the Chocolate Buttercream. Repeat with second layer. Top with last layer; spread top and side with remaining buttercream. Makes 16 servings.

CHOCOLATE BUTTERCREAM		
5	egg whites	5
1 cup	granulated sugar	250 mL
2 cups	unsalted butter, softened	500 mL
1-1/2 tsp	vanilla	7 mL
10 oz	bittersweet chocolate, melted and cooled	300 g

● In large bowl, whisk egg whites with sugar; place over saucepan of boiling water and whisk for about 2 minutes or until candy thermometer registers 110°F (43°C) or finger can remain in mixture for 10 seconds. Remove from heat.

● With heavy-duty mixer using whisk attachment or with electric mixer, beat at medium speed for 10 minutes or until very cool. Add butter, 1/4 cup (50 mL) at a time for first two additions and 1/2 cup (125 mL) at a time for remaining additions, beating until satiny and smooth. Beat in vanilla.

● On low speed, beat in cooled chocolate until no streaks remain. *(Buttercream can be covered with plastic wrap directly on surface and refrigerated for up to 5 days or frozen for up to 2 months; bring to room temperature, beating if necessary to recombine.)* Makes 5 cups (1.25 L).

TIP: To make icing the cake truly simple, use a cake turntable. You can garnish the iced cake with dark and white chocolate curls (see p. 88), piped buttercream rosettes or chocolate decorations.

Chocolate Hazelnut Dacquoise ▼

Dacquoise can be described as spectacular yet easy to make. The melt-in-your-mouth meringue layers are make-ahead, and the mousse, for all its French and fancy name, has no pitfalls in this era of modern appliances.

Per each of 16 servings: about
- 460 calories
- 33 g fat
- 7 g protein
- 40 g carbohydrate

2 cups	hazelnuts	500 mL
1-1/2 cups	granulated sugar	375 mL
1 tbsp	cornstarch	15 mL
6	egg whites	6
1 tsp	cream of tartar	5 mL
1/4 cup	sifted unsweetened cocoa powder	50 mL
	MOUSSE	
12 oz	semisweet chocolate, chopped	375 g
8	egg yolks	8
1/3 cup	granulated sugar	75 mL
1/4 cup	hazelnut-flavored liqueur (optional)	50 mL
2 cups	whipping cream	500 mL

● Toast hazelnuts on baking sheet in center of 350°F (180°C) oven for 5 to 10 minutes or until fragrant. Transfer to tea towel and rub off as much of the skins as possible; let cool.

● Meanwhile, line two 17- x 11-inch (45 x 29 cm) rimmed baking sheets with parchment paper or greased and floured foil. Using base of 8-inch (2 L) springform pan as guide, draw two circles on each sheet; turn paper over.

● In food processor, grind hazelnuts, 1/2 cup (125 mL) of the sugar and cornstarch until fine. In bowl, beat egg whites with cream of tartar until soft peaks form. Gradually beat in remaining sugar until glossy stiff peaks form. Fold in cocoa and half of the nut mixture. Fold in remaining nut mixture.

● Divide mixture among circles on baking sheets, spreading evenly. Bake in top and bottom thirds of 275°F (140°C) oven, switching and rotating pans halfway through, for about 2 hours or until crisp but not browned. Slide long metal spatula under meringues to loosen; transfer to rack and let cool completely. *(Meringues can be stored in waxed paper-lined tin in cool, dry place for up to 5 days.)*

● Break least attractive circle into coarse crumbs for garnish; store in airtight container. Using serrated knife and pan base as guide, trim remaining meringues into even circles.

● MOUSSE: In bowl over saucepan of hot (not boiling) water, melt chocolate, stirring occasionally. Remove from heat and keep warm. In top of double boiler over hot (not boiling) water, beat egg yolks with sugar on low speed for 3 minutes or until pale. Add liqueur (if using). Beat for 15 minutes or until pale and thickened. Remove from heat. Beat in melted chocolate. Whip cream; fold 1/2 cup (125 mL) into chocolate mixture. Fold in remaining whipped cream, one-third at a time.

● Place base of springform pan, rim side down, in pan. Line side with waxed paper collar that extends 1-1/2 inches (4 cm) above rim. Place one meringue circle in pan, flat side down. Set aside 1 cup (250 mL) of the mousse. Pour half of the remaining mousse into pan; spread to edge. Top with second meringue; spread with remaining mousse. Top with third meringue, flat side up, pressing lightly to level. Spread reserved mousse over top. Cover lightly with plastic wrap resting on paper collar; refrigerate for at least 4 hours or for up to 8 hours.

● Remove side of pan and collar. Sprinkle some of the reserved meringue crumbs in circle in center of top; press remaining pieces into side. Use metal spatula to gently slide cake off springform base onto serving platter. Makes 12 to 16 servings.

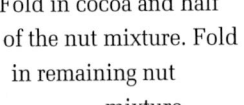

Chocolate Peanut Butter Mousse Cake

1/3 cup	chopped salted peanuts	75 mL
	CAKE	
1 cup	boiling water	250 mL
1/2 cup	unsweetened cocoa powder	125 mL
1-1/4 cups	all-purpose flour	300 mL
1 tsp	baking soda	5 mL
1/4 tsp	baking powder	1 mL
1/4 tsp	salt	1 mL
1/2 cup	butter, softened	125 mL
1 cup	granulated sugar	250 mL
2	eggs	2
1 tsp	vanilla	5 mL
	MOUSSE	
3/4 cup	smooth peanut butter	175 mL
1-1/2 cups	whipping cream	375 mL
2 tbsp	granulated sugar	25 mL
1/2 tsp	vanilla	2 mL
	GANACHE	
6 oz	bittersweet chocolate, chopped	175 g
2/3 cup	whipping cream	150 mL

● CAKE: In small bowl, whisk boiling water with cocoa until smooth; let cool to room temperature. In separate bowl, stir together flour, baking soda, baking powder and salt; set aside.

● In large bowl, beat butter with sugar until fluffy. Beat in eggs, one at a time, beating well after each addition. Beat in vanilla. With wooden spoon, stir in flour mixture alternately with cocoa mixture, making three additions of flour and two of cocoa.

● Pour into greased 9-inch (2.5 L) springform pan, smoothing top. Bake in center of 350°F (180°C) oven for 30 to 35 minutes or just until cake begins to pull away from side of pan and cake tester inserted in center comes out clean. Let cool in pan on rack for 20 minutes. Remove from pan. Let cool completely.

● MOUSSE: In bowl over saucepan of hot (not boiling) water, melt peanut butter; let stand until at room temperature yet still liquid.

● Meanwhile, place springform pan ring on freezer-safe cake plate. Cut 30- x 4-inch (76 x 10 cm) strip of waxed paper; fit around inside of ring. Fit cake back into pan.

● MOUSSE (continued): In bowl, whip together cream, sugar and vanilla; fold one-quarter into peanut butter until blended. Gently fold mixture back into remaining whipped cream until blended. Spoon over cake, spreading to cover and smoothing top. Cover lightly with plastic wrap; freeze for about 4 hours or until firm.

● GANACHE: Place chocolate in bowl. In saucepan, bring cream just to boil over medium heat; pour over chocolate, stirring, until melted. Let cool until at room temperature yet still pourable.

● Carefully remove ring from cake and peel off paper collar. Trim any raised edges from mousse to level top. Pour ganache over center of cake, spreading to edge and letting ganache flow down side randomly. Sprinkle ring of peanuts around top edge of cake.

● Freeze in rigid airtight container for about 1 hour or until ganache is set. *(Cake can be wrapped in plastic wrap or foil and frozen in rigid airtight container for up to 2 weeks. Let thaw in refrigerator for at least 6 hours or for up to 24 hours before serving.)* Or, serve *semifreddo*; thaw partially in refrigerator for about 2 hours. Makes 12 to 16 servings.

Chocolate plus — this time peanut butter, for an all-time, all-age favorite combination. The dark cake mates with a light-textured peanut butter mousse and is capped off with a glistening ganache.

Per each of 16 servings: about
- 400 calories
- 8 g protein
- 30 g fat
- 32 g carbohydrate

TIP: Use a palette knife to spread ganache over cake.

Chocolate Raspberry Dome ▶

This globe-shaped sensation features layers of dark and white chocolate mousse, a dramatic ganache polish and chocolate curls. With a smidgen of patience and a few licks of the bowl, the dome will come together successfully no matter what your baking experience.

Per serving: about
- 610 calories
- 42 g fat
- high source of fiber
- 10 g protein
- 60 g carbohydrate
- good source of iron

	White and dark chocolate curls (see p. 88)	
2 cups	fresh raspberries	500 mL
	SPONGE CAKE	
10	eggs, separated	10
2 cups	granulated sugar	500 mL
2 tsp	vanilla	10 mL
1 cup	all-purpose flour	250 mL
2/3 cup	unsweetened cocoa powder, sifted	150 mL
	DARK CHOCOLATE MOUSSE	
1	pkg (300 g) frozen unsweetened raspberries, thawed	1
2 tbsp	icing sugar	25 mL
12 oz	bittersweet or semisweet chocolate, chopped	375 g
2-1/2 cups	whipping cream	625 mL
	WHITE CHOCOLATE MOUSSE	
6 oz	white chocolate, chopped	175 g
1 tbsp	raspberry liqueur or kirsch	15 mL
3/4 cup	whipping cream	175 mL
	GANACHE	
6 oz	bittersweet chocolate, chopped	175 g
3/4 cup	whipping cream	175 mL

● Line two 17- x 11-inch (45 x 29 cm) rimmed baking sheets with parchment or waxed paper; set aside.

● SPONGE CAKE: In large bowl, beat 5 of the egg yolks with 1/2 cup (125 mL) of the sugar for 3 to 5 minutes or until pale and thickened. Beat in 1 tsp (5 mL) of the vanilla. Set aside. Combine 1/2 cup (125 mL) of the flour with 1/3 cup (75 mL) of the cocoa; set aside.

● In separate bowl, beat 5 of the egg whites until soft peaks form; gradually beat in 1/2 cup (125 mL) of the sugar until stiff peaks form. Spoon one-third over egg yolk mixture; sift one-third of the flour mixture over top and fold in. Repeat twice with remaining egg white and flour mixtures.

● Spread batter in one of the prepared pans, smoothing with palette knife or spatula. Bake in center of 400°F (200°C) oven for 12 minutes or until cake springs back when lightly touched. Let cool in pan on rack. Repeat with remaining ingredients to make second cake.

● DARK CHOCOLATE MOUSSE: Using wooden spoon, press raspberries and any juices through fine sieve into bowl to remove seeds. Whisk in icing sugar. Set purée aside.

● Place bittersweet chocolate in bowl. In saucepan, bring 1-1/2 cups (375 mL) of the cream just to boil over medium heat. Pour over chocolate, whisking until completely melted and smooth. Refrigerate all but 1/2 cup (125 mL) of the dark chocolate mixture for about 30 minutes or until slightly thickened and chilled.

● Meanwhile, with knife and using cake pans or cardboard templates as guides, cut 7-inch (18 cm) circle and 9-inch (23 cm) circle from one of the sponge cakes. From other cake, cut 5-inch (12 cm) circle and 11-inch (28 cm) circle, reserving scraps.

● Line 10-cup (2.5 L) bowl with plastic wrap. Fit largest cake circle snugly into bowl; peel off paper and smooth down cake. Line bowl to rim with reserved scraps.

● WHITE CHOCOLATE MOUSSE: In bowl over saucepan of hot (not boiling) water, melt white chocolate with raspberry liqueur and 1 tbsp (15 mL) water, stirring occasionally; let cool to room temperature. Whip cream; fold one-quarter into white chocolate. Gently fold in remaining whipped cream; set aside.

● Spread top of remaining cake circles with reserved 1/2 cup (125 mL) dark chocolate mixture; set aside.

● DARK CHOCOLATE MOUSSE (continued): Whisk 1/3 cup (75 mL) of the raspberry purée into chilled dark chocolate mixture. Cover and refrigerate remaining purée. Whip remaining 1 cup (250 mL) cream; fold one-third into dark chocolate mixture to lighten. Gently fold in remaining whipped cream to make dark chocolate mousse.

● Remove 1/2 cup (125 mL) of the dark chocolate mousse to small bowl; cover and refrigerate. Pour 1 cup (250 mL) of the remaining dark chocolate mousse into cake-lined bowl, smoothing with spatula. Top with 5-inch (12 cm) cake circle, glazed side down; peel off paper. Scatter 1 cup (250 mL) of the fresh raspberries over top. Pour white

chocolate mousse over top, smoothing with spatula. Top with 7-inch (18 cm) cake circle, glazed side down; peel off paper. Pour remaining dark chocolate mousse over cake, smoothing with spatula. Top with remaining cake circle, glazed side down; peel off paper. Cover with plastic wrap; refrigerate for at least 2 hours or for up to 24 hours.

● GANACHE: Place chocolate in bowl. In saucepan, bring cream just to boil over medium heat; pour over chocolate, whisking until completely melted. Let stand for 10 minutes.

● Meanwhile, remove plastic wrap from top of bowl and set rack on bowl. Invert bowl onto rack and place on rimmed

baking sheet. Gently lift off bowl; peel off plastic wrap.

● Let reserved dark chocolate mousse stand at room temperature for 10 minutes to soften; using palette knife, spread thin layer over dome. Starting at top of dome, pour ganache over cake in spiral motion, letting excess drip onto baking sheet and spreading with palette knife to cover completely. Refrigerate for at least 2 hours or for up to 10 hours.

● Transfer to serving plate. Garnish with white and dark chocolate curls and remaining raspberries. Serve with remaining raspberry purée. Makes 16 servings.

White Chocolate Carousel Cake ◄

3	eggs	3
1/2 cup	granulated sugar	125 mL
1/2 tsp	vanilla	2 mL
1/2 cup	all-purpose flour	125 mL
1/4 tsp	baking powder	1 mL
Pinch	salt	Pinch
3 tbsp	butter, melted	50 mL
	WHITE CHOCOLATE MOUSSE	
10 oz	white chocolate, chopped	285 g
3 tbsp	orange liqueur	50 mL
3 cups	strawberries, hulled	750 mL
1-1/2 cups	whipping cream	375 mL
	GARNISH	
1/4 cup	sliced almonds	50 mL
1/3 cup	apricot jam	75 mL
	Gold and silver candy-coated almonds	
	Candied violets	

● In bowl, beat eggs until foamy. Gradually beat in sugar; beat for 5 to 8 minutes or until batter falls in ribbons when beaters are lifted. Beat in vanilla.

● Stir together flour, baking powder and salt; sift half over egg mixture and fold in, using rubber spatula. Fold in remaining flour mixture. Remove one-quarter of the batter to small bowl; gradually fold in butter. Gradually fold back into batter.

● Scrape into greased 8-1/2-inch (2.25 L) springform pan. Bake in center of 325°F (160°C) oven for 40 minutes or until cake springs back when lightly pressed. Let cool in pan on rack for 20 minutes. Turn out onto rack; let cool completely.

● WHITE CHOCOLATE MOUSSE: In bowl over saucepan of hot (not boiling) water, melt together chocolate, liqueur and 2 tbsp (25 mL) water, stirring occasionally; let cool to room temperature.

● Place springform ring on platter. Cut 28- x 4-inch (71 x 10 cm) strip of waxed paper; fit around inside of ring. Trim top of cake if rounded; fit cake back into pan.

● Cut 12 large berries in half; arrange with tips up and cut sides against waxed-paper collar on top of cake. Snugly arrange remaining whole berries, tips up, to cover top of cake, making sure they are lower than top of halved berries.

● Whip cream; fold in white chocolate mixture in three additions. Pour over strawberries, spreading to cover berries; swirl top attractively. Cover lightly with plastic wrap; refrigerate for at least 4 hours or for up to 24 hours.

● GARNISH: Toast almonds on baking sheet in center of 350°F (180°C) oven for 5 to 10 minutes or until fragrant; let cool. Gently remove springform ring and peel off paper. In small saucepan, melt jam with 1 tbsp (15 mL) water; strain and brush over side of sponge cake only. Press toasted almonds into jam to adhere. Garnish top with candy-coated almonds and violets. Makes 12 servings.

VARIATION

● DARK CHOCOLATE MOUSSE CAROUSEL: For cake, reduce flour to 1/3 cup (75 mL); add 1/4 cup (50 mL) unsweetened cocoa powder along with flour. For mousse, substitute 8 oz (250 g) semisweet chocolate for white chocolate.

This is a big-impression cake, the centerpiece of a lavish dessert buffet or finale for a very special party. Like a lot of cakes that originate with professional bakers, the ingredients and steps for this spectacular cake may seem too complicated. However, do as pastry chefs do and prepare the cake layer ahead — it can be made up to 2 days ahead, and frozen for up to 2 weeks.

Per serving: about
- 385 calories
- 5 g protein
- 25 g fat
- 37 g carbohydrate

TIP: Use only good-quality white chocolate that has cocoa butter listed in the ingredients.

ELECTRIC MIXERS

An electric mixer is a godsend when making cakes. A good hand-held one with a power boost for long beating and heavy batters is good. If you bake a lot, investigate stand mixers — they free up your hands and mix batters more efficiently and quickly.

Cappuccino Torte ▼

Cooking teacher and author Jan Main marries an instant-cocoa mocha filling with mega cookie layers, then lets time mellow the torte to delectable, spoonable creaminess.

Per serving: about
- 475 calories
- 6 g protein
- 30 g fat
- 50 g carbohydrate

1 cup	butter, softened	250 mL
1 cup	granulated sugar	250 mL
2	eggs	2
2 cups	all-purpose flour	500 mL
4 tsp	cinnamon	20 mL
2 tsp	baking powder	10 mL
1/2 tsp	salt	2 mL
	FILLING	
2 cups	sour cream	500 mL
3/4 cup	granulated sugar	175 mL
1/2 cup	unsweetened cocoa powder	125 mL
1 tsp	each instant coffee granules and vanilla	5 mL
1 cup	whipping cream	250 mL
	GARNISH (OPTIONAL)	
	Coffee beans and sliced strawberries	

● Line two baking sheets with parchment paper. Using 9-inch (23 cm) round cake pan as guide, draw four circles on paper; turn paper over. Set aside.

● In bowl, beat butter with sugar until well combined; beat in eggs, one at a time, beating until fluffy. In separate bowl, stir together flour, cinnamon, baking powder and salt; beat into butter mixture, one-quarter at a time.

● Divide evenly among circles on baking sheets, spreading almost to edge with palette knife. Bake, one sheet at a time, in center of 350°F (180°C) oven for 15 to 20 minutes or until golden around edges. Let cookie layers cool on pan on rack.

● FILLING: In bowl, whisk together sour cream, sugar and cocoa. In small bowl, dissolve coffee granules in vanilla; whisk into sour cream mixture. In separate bowl, whip cream; fold into sour cream mixture. Refrigerate for 20 minutes or until chilled.

● Using palette knife, spread about one-quarter of the filling onto each cookie layer almost to edge; stack layers. Make swirls on top. Refrigerate for at least 6 hours or for up to 24 hours. *(Torte can be frozen, then wrapped in plastic wrap or foil and stored in rigid airtight container for up to 1 month.)*

● GARNISH (if using): Decorate with coffee beans and strawberries. Makes 12 servings.

Mocha Layer Cake

24	chocolate-covered coffee beans	24
	CAKE	
1/2 cup	sifted unsweetened cocoa powder	125 mL
1 tsp	baking soda	5 mL
1/2 cup	boiling water	125 mL
2 cups	sifted cake-and-pastry flour	500 mL
1 tsp	baking powder	5 mL
1/4 tsp	salt	1 mL
1/2 cup	unsalted butter, softened	125 mL
1-1/2 cups	granulated sugar	375 mL
2	eggs	2
1 tsp	vanilla	5 mL
1 cup	buttermilk	250 mL
	MOCHA CREAM	
2-1/4 cups	whipping cream	550 mL
1/3 cup	granulated sugar	75 mL
4 tsp	instant espresso powder or coffee granules	20 mL
1 tbsp	coffee liqueur (optional)	15 mL
	GANACHE	
2 oz	semisweet chocolate, chopped	60 g
1/4 cup	whipping cream	50 mL

● Grease 9-inch (2.5 L) springform pan; line bottom with waxed paper. Set aside.

● CAKE: In small bowl, combine cocoa and baking soda; gradually stir in water until smooth. Let cool completely. Sift together flour, baking powder and salt; set aside.

● In bowl, beat butter with sugar until combined. Beat in eggs, one at a time, beating well after each addition. Beat in vanilla, then cocoa mixture. With wooden spoon, stir in flour mixture alternately with buttermilk, making three additions of flour and two of buttermilk.

● Pour batter into prepared pan, smoothing top. Bake in center of 350°F (180°C) oven for 40 to 45 minutes or until center is set and side just begins to pull away from pan. Let cool on rack. Remove side of pan. Trim top with serrated knife, if necessary. *(Cake can be stored in airtight container for up to 2 days or wrapped in plastic wrap or foil and frozen in rigid airtight container for up to 1 month.)*

● MOCHA CREAM: In bowl, whip cream with sugar and espresso powder; blend in liqueur (if using). Set 1 cup (250 mL) aside for garnish.

● With serrated knife, cut cake horizontally into three layers; place bottom layer on cake plate. Slip strips of waxed paper underneath edge of cake to protect plate. Spread some of the mocha cream evenly over cake. Repeat with next layer. Top with remaining cake layer; spread remaining mocha cream over top and side. Remove paper strips. Refrigerate cake.

● GANACHE: Place chocolate in bowl. In saucepan, bring cream just to boil over medium heat; pour over chocolate, whisking until melted and smooth. Refrigerate for about 20 minutes or just until set but not firm. Using piping bag, pipe ganache decoratively over top of cake. (Alternatively, let ganache stand until cool but still liquid; drizzle over cake with fork.)

● Using piping bag fitted with star tip, pipe reserved mocha cream into rosettes around edge of cake. Place coffee beans on rosettes. Refrigerate for 1 hour. *(Cake can be refrigerated for up to 8 hours.)* Makes 12 to 16 servings.

What makes this cake special is its deep, chocolaty flavor and its cloak of mocha-flavored whipped cream.

Per each of 16 servings: about
- 370 calories
- 4 g protein
- 23 g fat
- 40 g carbohydrate

TIPS
● Because the Mocha Layer Cake is quite delicate, use the bottom of a tart pan to lift the individual layers during assembly.
● For a fine-textured cake, be sure to cool the cocoa-baking soda mixture completely before adding it to the batter.

WHIPPING CREAM

When whipping cream, be sure the bowl, beaters and cream are well chilled before starting. Pour the cream into the bowl and place in the freezer with the beaters for 10 minutes before whipping.

Nouvelle Bûche de Nöel ▶

A *bûche or Yule log is a classic in Quebec at Christmastime. Here's an occasion-making mascarpone mousse-filled log served with raspberry coulis. It was created by Montreal pastry chef Lesley Chesterman.*

Per serving (with Raspberry Coulis): about
- 440 calories
- 29 g fat
- 8 g protein
- 39 g carbohydrate

3	eggs	3
3	eggs, separated	3
3/4 cup	granulated sugar	175 mL
1 tsp	vanilla	5 mL
1/4 tsp	salt	1 mL
1/3 cup	unsweetened cocoa powder	75 mL
1/4 cup	all-purpose flour	50 mL
3 tbsp	icing sugar (approx)	50 mL
	Raspberry Coulis (recipe follows)	
	MASCARPONE MOUSSE	
1/4 cup	amaretto liqueur	50 mL
1-1/2 tsp	unflavored gelatin	7 mL
3	egg yolks	3
1/2 cup	icing sugar	125 mL
1 cup	mascarpone cheese	250 mL
1/2 cup	whipping cream	125 mL
	SYRUP	
3 tbsp	espresso or strong coffee	50 mL
2 tbsp	granulated sugar	25 mL
2 tbsp	dark rum or brandy	25 mL
	CHOCOLATE GANACHE	
4 oz	bittersweet chocolate, chopped	125 g
1/2 cup	whipping cream	125 mL
3 tbsp	unsalted butter, softened	50 mL
3 tbsp	icing sugar, sifted	50 mL

● In large bowl, beat together eggs, egg yolks and 1/2 cup (125 mL) of the granulated sugar for 5 to 7 minutes or until thick and cream-color. Blend in vanilla. In separate bowl, beat egg whites with salt until soft peaks form. Beat in remaining granulated sugar, 1 tbsp (15 mL) at a time, until stiff glossy peaks form; fold into yolk mixture. Sift cocoa with flour; fold into egg mixture in three additions.

● Spread in parchment or waxed paper-lined 17- x 11-inch (45 x 29 cm) rimmed baking sheet. Bake in center of 375°F (190°C) oven for 14 to 17 minutes or until top springs back when lightly touched. Let cool on rack for 5 minutes. Run knife around edge of pan to loosen. Sift icing sugar over clean tea towel; carefully invert cake onto towel. Remove paper. Trim edges with serrated knife, if necessary. Starting at long edge, immediately roll up cake in towel; let cool on rack.

● MASCARPONE MOUSSE: Pour amaretto into large bowl; sprinkle with gelatin. Let stand for about 5 minutes or until softened. Add egg yolks and icing sugar. Place over saucepan of simmering water; cook, whisking constantly, for 3 to 5 minutes or until thickened. Let cool slightly. Gradually beat in mascarpone cheese until smooth. Whip cream; fold into mascarpone mixture. Refrigerate for 10 to 15 minutes or until partially set.

● SYRUP: In saucepan, bring coffee and sugar to boil, stirring until sugar is dissolved. Remove from heat; let cool. Add rum. Set aside.

● CHOCOLATE GANACHE: Place chocolate in bowl. In saucepan, bring cream just to boil over medium heat; pour over chocolate, whisking until melted and smooth. Let stand at room temperature for about 1 hour or until thickened. Whisk in butter and icing sugar.

● Unroll cake; brush with syrup. Spread mousse over top. Using towel as support, tightly roll up cake. Place, seam side down, on platter. Cover and refrigerate for 30 minutes or until filling is set.

● Cut diagonal slice from each end of bûche. Spread top and sides with ganache. Arrange one cut piece on top of cake slightly off center and the other on one long side of cake to resemble cut branches; spread with ganache. Using fork or cake decorator comb, make shallow lengthwise ridges in ganache to resemble bark. Refrigerate for at least 1 hour or for up to 24 hours. *(Cake can be frozen until firm, then wrapped in plastic wrap or foil and stored in rigid airtight container for up to 1 month; let thaw in refrigerator for 24 hours.)*

● Let bûche stand at room temperature for 30 minutes before serving. Lightly sift more icing sugar over top. Spoon Raspberry Coulis onto serving plates; cut bûche into diagonal slices and arrange on top. Makes 12 servings.

RASPBERRY COULIS

2	pkg (each 300 g) frozen unsweetened raspberries, thawed	2
1/4 cup	granulated sugar	50 mL

● Drain raspberries, reserving 1/2 cup (125 mL) juice. Press through fine sieve set over bowl to remove seeds. Stir in sugar. Stir in enough reserved juice to make pourable. *(Coulis can be refrigerated in airtight container for up to 5 days.)* Makes about 1-1/2 cups (375 mL).

Per 2 tbsp (25 mL): about • 30 calories • trace protein • trace fat • 7 g carbohydrate

Light Chocolate Espresso Marble Cheesecake

How can a cheesecake be rich, creamy, satisfying — and light? The secret is cocoa, which is lower in fat than chocolate. So enjoy and leave all pangs of guilt at the door.

Per serving: about
- 215 calories
- 10 g fat
- 10 g protein
- 22 g carbohydrate

1/4 cup	chocolate wafer cookie crumbs (or 5 chocolate cookies, crushed)	50 mL
2 cups	1% cottage cheese	500 mL
1 cup	granulated sugar	250 mL
12 oz	light cream cheese, softened	375 g
2	eggs	2
1/2 cup	light sour cream	125 mL
2 tsp	vanilla	10 mL
1 tsp	cornstarch	5 mL
3 tbsp	unsweetened cocoa powder	50 mL
1/2 tsp	instant espresso powder or coffee granules	2 mL

● Line bottom of 8-inch (2 L) springform pan with parchment paper circle. Spray paper and side with nonstick cooking spray. Sprinkle crumbs over bottom. Center pan on large wide piece of foil; press foil tightly against side of pan. Set aside.

● In food processor, purée together cottage cheese and sugar, scraping down side of bowl twice, for about 45 seconds or until no longer granular. Add cream cheese; blend, scraping down side twice, until smooth.

Add eggs, one at a time, pulsing to combine. Add sour cream, vanilla and cornstarch; blend until smooth to form vanilla batter.

● In bowl, whisk together cocoa, espresso powder and 3 tbsp (50 mL) hot water until dissolved. Whisk in 2/3 cup (150 mL) of the vanilla batter. Pour half of the remaining vanilla batter into prepared pan. Spoon half of the chocolate batter randomly over top; using tip of knife, swirl batters together to create marble pattern. Pour remaining vanilla batter over top; spoon remaining chocolate batter on top. Repeat swirling to create marble pattern.

● Set pan in larger pan; pour in enough hot water to come 1 inch (2.5 cm) up sides. Bake in center of 325°F (160°C) oven for about 1 hour or just until set around edge yet still jiggly in center. Turn off oven; run knife around edge of cake. Let stand in oven for 1 hour.

● Transfer springform pan to rack and remove foil; let cool completely. Cover with plastic wrap and refrigerate for at least 8 hours or for up to 2 days. Serve in thin wedges. Makes 12 servings.

TIP: To serve, simply slide cheesecake away from the parchment-paper lining.

Chocolate Cookie Cheesecake ▶

A cool, creamy, chock-full-of-chocolate cheesecake, with a whimsical cut-cookie topping, tastes just as great as it looks.

Per each of 12 servings: about
- 495 calories
- 36 g fat
- 8 g protein
- 37 g carbohydrate

3	pkg (250 g each) cream cheese, softened	3
3/4 cup	granulated sugar	175 mL
3	eggs	3
1 tsp	vanilla	5 mL
1 cup	sour cream	250 mL
2 tsp	all-purpose flour	10 mL
15	chocolate sandwich cream cookies, broken in small pieces	15

	CRUST	
15	chocolate sandwich cream cookies	15
3 tbsp	butter, melted	50 mL
	GARNISH	
7	chocolate sandwich cream cookies	7

● CRUST: In food processor or blender, crush cookies to fine crumbs; blend in butter until crumbs are moistened. With back of spoon, press onto bottom and 1/4 inch (5 mm) up side of lightly greased 8-1/2-inch (2.25 L) springform pan. Center pan on large piece of foil; press foil tightly against side of pan. Set aside in refrigerator.

● In bowl, beat cream cheese until smooth. Beat in sugar until fluffy. Beat in eggs, one at a time, beating well after each addition. Beat in vanilla, then sour cream and flour.

● Pour one-third over prepared crust; sprinkle with half of the broken cookies. Repeat once. Top with remaining batter, smoothing top.

● Set pan in larger pan; pour in enough hot water to come 1 inch (2.5 cm) up sides. Bake in center of 325°F (160°C) oven for 50 to 60 minutes or until set around edge yet still jiggly in center.

Turn off oven; run knife around edge of cake. Let stand in oven for 1 hour.

● Transfer springform pan to rack and remove foil; let cool completely. Cover with plastic wrap and refrigerate for at least 8 hours or for up to 3 days.

● GARNISH: Just before serving, remove cake from pan and base. Cut cookies in half; arrange on cake. Makes 10 to 12 servings.

Dark Chocolate Cheesecake

Associate food director
Daphna Rabinovitch
launched the Canadian Living
Cooking School with a series
of chocolate workshops
showcasing recipes such as
this dark and devilish
cheesecake she created
especially for it.

Per serving: about
- 330 calories
- 25 g fat
- 6 g protein
- 26 g carbohydrate

12 oz	bittersweet chocolate, chopped	375 g
1 tbsp	instant espresso powder or coffee granules	15 mL
2	pkg (250 g each) cream cheese, softened	2
3/4 cup	granulated sugar	175 mL
3	eggs	3
2 tsp	vanilla	10 mL
Pinch	salt	Pinch
1 cup	sour cream	250 mL
	CRUST	
1 cup	chocolate wafer cookie crumbs	250 mL
2 tbsp	butter, melted	25 mL

● CRUST: Stir crumbs with butter until well moistened. Press onto bottom of greased 8-1/2-inch (2.25 L) springform pan. Center pan on large square of foil; press foil tightly against side of pan. Bake in center of 325°F (160°C) oven for 10 minutes or until set. Let cool.

● In bowl over saucepan of hot (not boiling) water, melt chocolate, stirring occasionally; let cool to room temperature. Dissolve espresso powder in 1 tbsp (15 mL) hot water; set aside.

● Meanwhile, in large bowl, beat cream cheese until smooth. Beat in sugar, 1/4 cup (50 mL) at a time; beat for 3 minutes or until light and smooth, scraping down bowl often. On low speed, beat in eggs, one at a time, beating well after each addition and scraping down bowl often. Beat in vanilla and salt. With spatula, blend in sour cream, chocolate and espresso mixture until no streaks remain. Pour onto prepared crust.

● Set pan in larger pan; pour in enough hot water to come 1 inch (2.5 cm) up sides. Bake in center of 325°F (160°C) oven for about 45 minutes or until set around edge yet still jiggly in center. Turn off oven; run knife around edge of cake. Let stand in oven for 1 hour.

● Transfer springform pan to rack and remove foil; let cool completely. Cover with plastic wrap and refrigerate for at least 12 hours or for up to 2 days. *(Cheesecake can be wrapped in plastic wrap and frozen in rigid airtight container for up to 1 week.)* Makes 16 servings.

TIP: To make 1 cup (250 mL) chocolate crumbs, place about 23 chocolate wafer cookies (100 g) in food processor or plastic bag and crush until in fine crumbs.

Chocolate Pavlova ▶

"Elegant" perfectly
describes this crisp-on-the-
outside, marshmallow-soft-
on-the-inside puff, crowned
luxuriously with cream,
strawberries and a drizzle of
bittersweet chocolate.

Per each of 8 servings: about
- 390 calories
- 21 g fat
- 5 g protein
- 51 g carbohydrate

6	egg whites	6		TOPPING		
1/4 tsp	salt	1 mL	3 cups	strawberries, hulled	750 mL
1/4 tsp	cream of tartar	1 mL	1-1/2 cups	whipping cream	375 mL
1-1/2 cups	granulated sugar	375 mL	2 tsp	granulated sugar	10 mL
3 tbsp	unsweetened cocoa powder	50 mL	1 oz	bittersweet chocolate, melted	30 g
2 tsp	cornstarch	10 mL			
1 tbsp	vinegar	15 mL			
2 tsp	vanilla	10 mL			
2 oz	bittersweet chocolate, chopped	60 g			

● Line rimmed baking sheet with parchment paper or greased and floured foil. Using 8-inch (20 cm) cake pan as guide, draw circle on paper; turn paper over.

● In bowl, beat together egg whites, salt and cream of tarter until soft peaks form. Beat in sugar, about 3 tbsp (50 mL) at a time, until stiff glossy peaks form. Sift cocoa and cornstarch over top; gently fold in. Gently fold in vinegar, vanilla, then chocolate.

● Mound onto circle on prepared baking sheet. Bake in center of 275°F (140°C) oven for 1-1/2 hours or until

crispy outside but still soft in center. Slide long metal spatula under meringue to loosen; transfer to rack and let cool completely. Place on serving platter.

● TOPPING: Slice or halve strawberries. In bowl, whip cream with sugar; spread over meringue. Arrange strawberries decoratively over top. Drizzle chocolate over berries. Makes 6 to 8 servings.

TIPS

● Eggs separate better when cold but beat up to a higher volume when at room temperature.
● If you have no bittersweet chocolate on hand to drizzle over the berries, just sieve some unsweetened cocoa powder over top for a dazzling effect.

Chocolate Tiramisu Torte

From the kitchen of Marianne Sanders, Calgary dessert star, comes this elegant cake, its chocolate-coffee-flavored layers melded together with rich chocolate ganache and mascarpone cream. All the flavors of tiramisu in a delicious fork version!

Per serving: about
- 570 calories
- 10 g protein
- 46 g fat
- 42 g carbohydrate
- excellent source of iron

7 oz	bittersweet chocolate, chopped	210 g
1/4 cup	double-strength coffee	50 mL
7	eggs, separated	7
3/4 cup	granulated sugar	175 mL
	CHOCOLATE GANACHE FILLING	
5 oz	bittersweet chocolate, chopped	150 g
3/4 cup	whipping cream	175 mL
1/4 cup	coffee	50 mL
	MASCARPONE FILLING	
1	tub (250 g) mascarpone cheese	1
1/2 cup	whipping cream	125 mL
2 tbsp	rum	25 mL
	BRUSHING LIQUID	
1 tbsp	coffee	15 mL
1 tbsp	rum	15 mL
	CHOCOLATE WRAP	
6 oz	bittersweet chocolate, chopped	175 g
2 tsp	corn syrup	10 mL

● In bowl over saucepan of hot (not boiling) water, melt chocolate, stirring occasionally. Stir in coffee; let cool.

● In large bowl, whisk egg yolks with 1/2 cup (125 mL) of the sugar; whisk in melted chocolate. Set aside. In separate bowl, beat egg whites until soft peaks form; beat in remaining sugar, 2 tbsp (25 mL) at a time, until stiff peaks form. Stir one-third of the egg whites into chocolate mixture; fold in remaining whites.

● Spread on parchment or waxed paper-lined 17- x 11-inch (45 x 29 cm) rimmed baking sheet. Bake in center of 350°F (180°C) oven for 20 to 25 minutes or until crusty on top. Let cool. *(Cake and pan can be wrapped in plastic wrap and set aside for up to 1 day.)*

● Invert cake onto waxed paper-lined tray; peel off paper. Trim rough edges to make 16- x 10-1/2-inch (40 x 26 cm) rectangle. Cut lengthwise in half; cut crosswise in half to form four layers.

● CHOCOLATE GANACHE FILLING: In bowl over saucepan of hot (not boiling) water, melt chocolate with cream and coffee, whisking until smooth and glossy. Cover and refrigerate for about 3 hours or until chilled; beat until fluffy. *(Ganache can be refrigerated in airtight container for up to 5 days.)*

● MASCARPONE FILLING: In bowl, beat together mascarpone cheese, cream and rum until stiff and airy.

● BRUSHING LIQUID: Stir coffee with rum; brush about one-quarter over first cake layer. Spread with half of the mascarpone filling. Top with second cake layer; brush with a little more coffee mixture. Spread top with half of the ganache filling. Repeat with remaining cake, mascarpone filling and ganache to form four layers. *(Torte can be prepared to this point, wrapped in plastic wrap and refrigerated for up to 24 hours.)*

● CHOCOLATE WRAP: Using waxed paper, cut out pattern 1/2 inch (1 cm) larger on all sides than top of cake. Using another piece of waxed paper, cut out four separate pieces to match ends and sides of cake, making them 1/2 inch (1 cm) taller than cake.

● In bowl over saucepan of hot (not boiling) water, melt chocolate, stirring occasionally. Stir in corn syrup. Using spatula, spread about half of the chocolate mixture over pattern for top; place, waxed-paper side up, on cake. Refrigerate for about 10 minutes or until set. Peel off paper. Repeat for ends and sides, letting chocolate extend at top. *(Torte can be refrigerated in airtight container for up to 2 days.)*

● To serve, let torte stand at room temperature for 10 minutes or until chocolate is soft enough to slice without splintering. Makes 10 servings.

Chocolate Cake Finishes

*Food stylist Ruth Gangbar offers two amazing — and amazingly easy — ways to make your favorite
two-layer cake (or Three-Layer Chocolate Fudge Cake, p. 6) into a work of art. To showcase the chocolate,
ice the cake with our creamy white Basic Butter Icing (p. 24).*

Chocolate Shell

Wrap a cake in chocolate, then tie it with a festive ribbon.

● Measure a piece of parchment paper to fit around cake, allowing enough for a little overlap and to extend 1 inch (2.5 cm) above top.

● In bowl over saucepan of hot (not boiling) water, melt 8 oz (250 g) chopped bittersweet chocolate; let cool slightly. With palette knife, spread chocolate evenly over paper. Place on inverted baking sheet. Refrigerate until chocolate is firm and beginning to lose its shine at the edges yet is still sticky to the touch.

● Carefully lift paper and chocolate; press chocolate around cake, crimping gently. To make it easier, ask a friend to hold one end of the chocolate and paper, or prepare shorter lengths at separate intervals (so they don't all harden at once), and overlap them when pressing lengths around cake.

● Let chocolate harden completely; gently peel off paper. Dust cake with cocoa powder.

Patterns in Chocolate

Be creative when making a pattern, or template, with cutout shapes using an X-acto knife and cardboard or plastic container lids. Paper doilies or even interesting foliage make nice patterns, too.

● Chill the cake so that the icing is cold, which means a less sticky surface for easy removal of the pattern.

● Insert straight pins upward through the pattern for "handles." Position the pattern onto the iced cake, then dust with cocoa powder. Using the pin handles, lift the pattern and turn it slightly. Dust again with icing sugar.

Chocolate Pecan Fruitcake

Something old, something new — chocolate adds a delightfully unexpected twist to a fine old-fashioned fruitcake.

Per slice: about
- 115 calories
- 1 g protein
- 5 g fat
- 17 g carbohydrate

4-1/2 cups	mixed candied pineapple and cherries (about 2 lb/1 kg)	1.125 L
2 cups	coarsely chopped toasted pecans	500 mL
4 oz	unsweetened chocolate, chopped	125 g
3 oz	semisweet chocolate, chopped	90 g
1 cup	golden raisins	250 mL
2 cups	all-purpose flour	500 mL
2 tsp	baking powder	10 mL
1/2 tsp	salt	2 mL
3/4 cup	unsalted butter, softened	175 mL
1 cup	granulated sugar	250 mL
6	eggs	6
3/4 cup	brandy	175 mL
1 tsp	vanilla	5 mL

● In large bowl, toss together pineapple, cherries, pecans, unsweetened and semisweet chocolate and raisins. Add 1 cup (250 mL) of the flour; toss to coat fruit evenly. Stir together remaining flour, baking powder and salt; set aside.

● In large bowl, beat butter with sugar until light and fluffy; beat in eggs, one at a time, beating well after each addition. Beat in 1/4 cup (50 mL) of the brandy and vanilla. Stir in dry ingredients, about 1/3 cup (75 mL) at a time, until well blended. Stir in fruit mixture.

● Scrape batter into greased 13- x 9-inch (3.5 L) cake pan, spreading evenly and tapping pan on counter to eliminate air pockets. Bake in center of 300°F (150°C) oven for 1-1/2 hours or until cake tester inserted in center comes out clean. Let cool in pan on rack.

● Cut cake crosswise into 6 bars. With skewer, make several holes through cake. Heat remaining brandy just until hot but not boiling; pour over cake.

● Moisten pieces of cheesecloth with brandy; wrap around individual bars. Wrap in waxed paper, then foil; store in airtight container in cool, dry place for at least 1 week or for up to 2 months, checking occasionally and adding more brandy if cake begins to dry. Makes 6 small cakes, about 14 slices each.

TIP: It's easy to slice fruitcake if you refrigerate it a few hours before serving. Always slice with a very sharp knife and wipe the blade with a damp cloth between slices.

ALL-OCCASION BUTTER ICINGS

Basic Butter Icing

● In bowl, beat 1 cup (250 mL) softened butter at medium speed until light. Gradually beat in 5 cups (1.25 L) icing sugar and 2/3 cup (150 mL) whipping cream, making three additions of sugar and two of cream. *(Butter icing can be covered and refrigerated for up to 3 days; beat again before using.)* Makes about 4 cups (1 L).

Best-Ever Chocolate Icing

● In bowl over saucepan of hot (not boiling) water, melt 6 oz (175 g) chopped unsweetened chocolate, stirring occasionally. Let cool.
● In separate bowl, beat 1-1/2 cups (375 mL) softened unsalted butter until fluffy; beat in 1/2 cup (125 mL) whipping cream, 2 tbsp (25 mL) at a time. Beat in 1 tbsp (15 mL) vanilla. Beat in 3 cups (750 mL) icing sugar, 1 cup (250 mL) at a time. Beat in melted chocolate until icing is fluffy and smooth. Makes 5 cups (1.25 L).

Chocolate Brownie Turtle Cake ▼

4 oz	each semisweet and unsweetened chocolate, chopped	125 g
3/4 cup	butter	175 mL
3	eggs	3
1-1/2 cups	granulated sugar	375 mL
1 tsp	vanilla	5 mL
3/4 cup	all-purpose flour	175 mL
3/4 tsp	baking powder	4 mL
Pinch	salt	Pinch
3/4 cup	chopped pecans	175 mL
3/4 cup	chocolate chips or chopped semisweet chocolate (optional)	175 mL
	CARAMEL LAYER	
10 oz	light caramels	300 g
2 tbsp	whipping cream	25 mL
	GLAZE AND GARNISH	
6 oz	semisweet chocolate, chopped	175 g
1/3 cup	whipping cream	75 mL
12	pecan halves	12

● In bowl over saucepan of hot (not boiling) water, melt together semisweet and unsweetened chocolate and butter, stirring occasionally. Let cool.

● In large bowl, whisk together eggs, sugar and vanilla until well combined. Stir in chocolate mixture. Mix together flour, baking powder and salt; stir into chocolate mixture. Add pecans, and chocolate chips (if using), stirring just until combined.

● Scrape into greased 9-inch (2.5 L) springform pan. Bake in center of 350°F (180°C) oven for 45 minutes or just until cake starts to pull away from side and cracks on top. Let cool in pan on rack.

● CARAMEL LAYER: In small bowl over saucepan of simmering water, melt caramels with cream, stirring occasionally, for 10 minutes or until smooth. Pour over cake in pan. Refrigerate for 30 minutes or until caramel is set.

● GLAZE AND GARNISH: In bowl over saucepan of hot (not boiling) water, melt chocolate with cream, stirring occasionally. Let cool slightly; pour over caramel layer. Garnish with pecans. Refrigerate for at least 4 hours or for up to 24 hours. *(Cake can be wrapped in plastic wrap or foil in pan and frozen in airtight container for up to 2 weeks. Thaw in refrigerator for 5 hours.)*

● To serve, remove side from pan and transfer cake to serving platter; let stand at room temperature for 15 minutes. Makes 12 to 16 servings.

A *dense, rich chocolate cake, studded with pecans and chocolate chips, comes topped with caramel and, if that wasn't enough, a chocolate glaze and nut finish!*

Per each of 16 servings: about
- 450 calories
- 28 g fat
- 5 g protein
- 50 g carbohydrate

Chocolate Indulgence Cake

*Satisfy chocolate cravings
with a mere sliver of this
super-dense cake, adapted
from a dessert sensation at
Stars in San Francisco.*

Per serving: about
- 500 calories
- 9 g protein
- 40 g fat
- 40 g carbohydrate
- good source
  of iron

TIP: If you wish, serve half
slices accompanied with
berries.

8 oz	bittersweet chocolate, chopped	250 g
1 tbsp	butter	15 mL
2 tbsp	instant coffee granules	25 mL
2 tsp	vanilla	10 mL
7	eggs, separated	7
2/3 cup	granulated sugar	150 mL
	GANACHE	
1 lb	bittersweet chocolate, chopped	500 g
2 cups	whipping cream	500 mL

● GANACHE: Place chocolate in bowl. In
saucepan, bring cream just to boil over
medium heat; pour over chocolate, whisking
until melted and smooth. Cover with plastic
wrap and refrigerate for about 1 hour or until
cooled and thickened but still pourable.

● Line two 15- x 10-inch (40 x 25 cm)
rimmed baking sheets with parchment or
waxed paper; set aside.

● In bowl over saucepan of hot (not boiling)
water, melt chocolate with butter, stirring
occasionally. Remove from heat. Dissolve
coffee in vanilla; whisk into chocolate
mixture along with egg yolks until smooth.
Let stand at room temperature for 5 to
10 minutes or until cooled slightly.

● In separate bowl, beat egg whites until soft
peaks form. Beat in sugar, 2 tbsp (25 mL) at
a time, until stiff peaks form; fold one-third
into chocolate mixture to lighten. Fold in
remaining egg whites in two additions.
Divide batter between prepared pans,
smoothing with palette knife.

● Bake in top and bottom thirds of 375°F
(190°C) oven, rotating pans halfway through,
for 12 to 15 minutes or until tops look dry
and cakes spring back when lightly touched.
Transfer to racks and let cool completely.

● Run knife around sides of pans to loosen
cakes; slide onto cutting board. Place
8- x 4-inch (1.5 L) loaf pan on top of one of
the cakes at one short end. With knife, trace
base, cutting through cake and parchment
paper. Repeat twice on same cake. Repeat
with second cake to make six layers.

● Line bottom of loaf pan with parchment or
waxed paper. Pour in 1/2 cup (125 mL) of the
ganache. Invert one cake layer onto ganache;
carefully peel off paper. (Cake may crack
slightly.) Pour another 1/2 cup (125 mL) of
the ganache over cake, tilting pan back and
forth to cover completely. Repeat layers
four more times; top with remaining cake
layer.

● Cover cake with plastic wrap and refrigerate
for at least 6 hours or until set. Cover and
refrigerate remaining ganache. *(Cake and
remaining ganache can be refrigerated for up
to 2 days.)*

● Remove plastic wrap. Run knife around
pan to loosen cake. Invert onto serving plate;
peel off paper. Using palette knife, smooth
sides and top, if necessary. Spoon remaining
ganache into pastry bag fitted with small
rosette tip. Pipe border of small rosettes
around top and bottom. Cut into thin slices to
serve. Makes 12 servings.

Chocolate Walnut Cake

8 oz	semisweet chocolate, chopped	250 g
12	eggs, separated	12
1 cup	granulated sugar	250 mL
1/4 tsp	salt	1 mL
2 cups	finely ground walnuts	500 mL
3 tbsp	all-purpose flour	50 mL
1 tbsp	icing sugar	15 mL

● In bowl over saucepan of hot (not boiling) water, melt chocolate, stirring occasionally. Remove from heat and let cool slightly.

● In large bowl, beat egg yolks with 1/2 cup (125 mL) of the granulated sugar for about 3 minutes or just until starting to thicken. Add chocolate; beat until thoroughly blended.

● In separate large bowl, beat egg whites with salt until soft but definite peaks form; gradually beat in remaining granulated sugar until stiff glossy peaks form. Fold one-third into chocolate mixture; repeat with another third. Stir together nuts and flour; fold into mixture along with remaining egg whites.

● Pour batter into ungreased 10-inch (4 L) tube pan. Bake in center of 350°F (180°C) oven for 60 to 65 minutes or until cake tester inserted in center comes out clean.

● Turn pan upside down and let hang on legs attached to pan or on inverted funnel or bottle until completely cool. Run thin paring knife around edge of cake to unmould from pan. *(Cake can be frozen in rigid airtight container for up to 1 week; let thaw at room temperature.)*

● Place cake on serving platter; sift icing sugar over top. Makes 16 servings.

This nutty, light-textured cake proves that a chocolate cake doesn't have to be dense and creamy to be intensely flavored and really satisfying.

Per serving: about
- 250 calories
- 7 g protein
- 15 g fat
- 24 g carbohydrate

TIP: For fresh walnut flavor, choose only California walnuts. You will need 10 oz (300 g), then grind them in the food processor. Or buy them already ground.

Chocolate Chip Coffee Cake

2 cups	all-purpose flour	500 mL
3/4 cup	granulated sugar	175 mL
1 tbsp	baking powder	15 mL
1 tsp	baking soda	5 mL
1/4 tsp	salt	1 mL
1	egg	1
1 cup	2% evaporated milk	250 mL
2 tbsp	vegetable oil	25 mL
2 tsp	vanilla	10 mL
	FILLING	
1/4 cup	coarsely chopped pecans	50 mL
1 cup	chocolate chips (6 oz/175 g)	250 mL
1/4 cup	packed brown sugar	50 mL
2 tsp	cinnamon	10 mL

● FILLING: Toast pecans on baking sheet in center of 350°F (180°C) oven for 5 minutes or until lightly browned; let cool. In bowl, combine toasted pecans, chocolate chips, brown sugar and cinnamon; set aside.

● In separate bowl, stir together flour, sugar, baking powder, baking soda and salt. In another bowl, whisk together egg, milk, oil and vanilla; pour over flour mixture and stir just until blended.

● Spread half of the batter in greased 10-inch (3 L) Bundt pan. Sprinkle with half of the filling. Top with remaining batter; sprinkle remaining filling over top, lightly pressing chocolate chips and nuts into batter.

● Bake in center of 350°F (180°C) oven for 45 to 60 minutes or until cake tester inserted in center comes out clean. Let cool in pan on rack. Turn out onto serving plate, with chocolate and nuts on top. Makes 12 servings.

Especially for all those brunch and morning-coffee occasions comes this fat-reduced coffee cake. Serve very fresh to appreciate the crunchy pecans and melting chocolate chips.

Per serving: about
- 280 calories
- 5 g protein
- 10 g fat
- 45 g carbohydrate

Chocolate Cloud Cake

Serious chocoholics will swoon over this creation that's more fudge than cake. A burst of orange and whipped cream helps keep our chocolate feet on the ground. Our thanks to dessert guru Richard Sax and his cloud cake for the inspiration.

Per serving: about
- 355 calories
- 5 g protein
- 27 g fat
- 29 g carbohydrate

8 oz	bittersweet chocolate, chopped	250 g
1/2 cup	unsalted butter	125 mL
3	eggs	3
1 cup	granulated sugar	250 mL
2 tbsp	orange liqueur	25 mL
1-1/2 tsp	grated orange rind	7 mL
3	egg whites	3
	TOPPING	
1-1/2 cups	whipping cream	375 mL
2 tbsp	icing sugar	25 mL
1/2 tsp	vanilla	2 mL

● Line bottom of ungreased 8-inch (2 L) springform pan with waxed paper; set aside.

● In bowl over saucepan of hot (not boiling) water, melt chocolate with butter, stirring occasionally. Let cool slightly.

● In separate bowl, whisk whole eggs with half of the sugar just until turning pale and starting to thicken; whisk in chocolate mixture, liqueur and orange rind.

● In another bowl, beat egg whites until soft peaks form; gradually beat in remaining sugar, 2 tbsp (25 mL) at a time, until stiff shiny peaks form. Fold one-quarter into chocolate mixture; fold in remaining whites in two additions.

● Pour into prepared pan. Bake in center of 350°F (180°C) oven for 45 to 50 minutes or until top is puffed and starting to crack but center still looks wet. Let cool completely in pan on rack (center will fall, leaving higher sides). *(Cake can be wrapped in plastic wrap and refrigerated for up to 2 days or over-wrapped in foil and frozen for up to 2 weeks.)* Run knife around cake to loosen; carefully unmould onto cake plate.

● TOPPING: In bowl, whip cream with sugar and vanilla; mound in center of cake, swirling lightly. To serve, cut with wet hot knife. Makes 12 servings.

TIP: If desired, garnish with strips of orange rind or sieve cocoa powder over top (sprinkling could result in uneven coating).

Chocolate Prune Rum Cake ▶

We're used to matching chocolate with fresh berries, oranges and bananas — but prunes? Yes, for the way they deepen and enrich the chocolate flavor and provide the cake with preserving qualities.

Per serving: about
- 380 calories
- 6 g protein
- 22 g fat
- 46 g carbohydrate
- good source of iron
- high source of fiber

2 cups	pitted prunes, chopped	500 mL
1/4 cup	dark rum	50 mL
2 tsp	instant coffee granules	10 mL
8 oz	bittersweet chocolate, chopped	250 g
1 tsp	grated orange rind	5 mL
1/4 cup	orange juice	50 mL
1 cup	butter, softened	250 mL
1 cup	granulated sugar	250 mL
5	eggs, separated	5
2 cups	all-purpose flour	500 mL
1 tsp	cinnamon	5 mL
1/4 tsp	each salt and cream of tartar	1 mL

	CHOCOLATE GLAZE	
4 oz	bittersweet chocolate, chopped	125 g
1 tbsp	dark rum	15 mL
2 tsp	instant coffee granules	10 mL

● In saucepan, combine prunes and rum; cover and cook over low heat for 5 minutes. Set aside.

● In small bowl, dissolve instant coffee in 1 tbsp (15 mL) hot water. In separate bowl over saucepan of hot (not boiling) water, melt chocolate, stirring occasionally. Stir in coffee and orange rind and juice. Set aside.

● In large bowl, beat butter with sugar until fluffy; beat in egg yolks until light. Beat in chocolate mixture, prune mixture, flour and cinnamon.

● In separate bowl, beat egg whites with salt and cream of tartar until stiff peaks form. Fold one-third into batter; fold in remaining whites. Scrape into greased 10-inch (3 L) Bundt pan.

● Bake in center of 350°F (180°C) oven for 50 to 60 minutes or until firm to the touch and cake tester inserted in center comes out clean. Let cool in pan on rack. Turn out onto serving plate. *(Cake can be prepared to this point, wrapped in plastic wrap or foil and refrigerated for up to 1 week.)*

● CHOCOLATE GLAZE: Place chocolate in bowl. In small saucepan, bring 3 tbsp (50 mL) hot water, rum and instant coffee to boil; boil for 1 minute. Pour over chocolate, stirring until melted. Drizzle over cake. Makes 16 servings.

Easy Chocolate Snacking Cake

Anne Lindsay made over a typical chocolate cake into this moist and much lighter version.

Per serving: about
- 270 calories
- 6 g fat
- 5 g protein
- 51 g carbohydrate

2 tbsp	instant espresso powder or coffee granules	25 mL
1/2 cup	boiling water	125 mL
2-1/4 cups	all-purpose flour	550 mL
2 cups	granulated sugar	500 mL
3/4 cup	unsweetened cocoa powder	175 mL
1-1/2 tsp	each baking powder and baking soda	7 mL
1 tsp	salt	5 mL
1-3/4 cups	buttermilk	425 mL
2	eggs	2
1/4 cup	vegetable oil	50 mL
2 tsp	vanilla	10 mL
	CHOCOLATE ICING	
1/2 cup	unsweetened cocoa powder	125 mL
1/4 cup	granulated sugar	50 mL
4 tsp	cornstarch	20 mL
1/2 cup	buttermilk	125 mL
1/4 cup	corn syrup	50 mL
1/2 tsp	vanilla	2 mL

● Dissolve espresso powder in water; let cool. Grease 13- x 9-inch (3.5 L) cake pan; line bottom with waxed paper.

● In large bowl, mix together flour, sugar, cocoa, baking powder, baking soda and salt. Beat in buttermilk, eggs, oil, vanilla and espresso mixture; beat for 2 minutes. Pour into prepared pan.

● Bake in center of 350°F (180°C) oven for about 45 minutes or until top springs back when lightly touched. Let cool in pan on rack for 20 minutes. Remove from pan; let cool completely on rack.

● CHOCOLATE ICING: Meanwhile, in heavy saucepan, mix together cocoa, sugar and cornstarch; whisk in buttermilk and corn syrup until smooth. Whisking constantly, bring to simmer over medium heat; simmer for 2 minutes. Remove from heat; stir in vanilla. Let cool, stirring occasionally, for 45 minutes or until thickened. Spread over top and sides of cake. Makes 16 servings.

Choco-Chip Buttermilk Loaf

The combination of cocoa, buttermilk and soda ensures a loaf cake with a tender, even crumb. Try wrapping individual slices to sell at the next bake sale — they're sure to sell out fast.

Per serving: about
- 340 calories
- 18 g fat
- 5 g protein
- 42 g carbohydrate

3/4 cup	butter, softened	175 mL
1 cup	granulated sugar	250 mL
2	eggs	2
2 tsp	vanilla	10 mL
1/2 tsp	grated orange rind	2 mL
2 cups	all-purpose flour	500 mL
1/4 cup	unsweetened cocoa powder	50 mL
1 tsp	baking soda	5 mL
1/2 tsp	salt	2 mL
2/3 cup	buttermilk	150 mL
1 cup	semisweet chocolate chips	250 mL

● Grease 9- x 5-inch (2 L) loaf pan. Line bottom with parchment or waxed paper; set aside.

● In large bowl, beat butter with sugar until light and fluffy; beat in eggs, one at a time, beating well after each addition. Beat in vanilla and orange rind. In separate bowl, stir together flour, cocoa, baking soda and salt; add to butter mixture alternately with buttermilk, making three additions of flour mixture and two of buttermilk. Stir in chocolate chips.

● Scrape batter into prepared pan, smoothing top. Bake in center of 350°F (180°C) oven for about 1 hour or until cake tester inserted in center comes out clean. Let cool in pan for 10 minutes; turn out onto rack and remove paper. Let cool completely. *(Cake can be wrapped in plastic wrap or foil and frozen in rigid airtight container for up to 1 month. Thaw completely at room temperature before slicing.)* Makes 12 servings.

Chocolate Espresso Angel Cake

1-1/4 cups	sifted cake-and-pastry flour	300 mL
1-1/2 cups	granulated sugar	375 mL
1-1/2 cups	egg whites (about 11), at room temperature	375 mL
1 tbsp	lemon juice	15 mL
1 tsp	cream of tartar	5 mL
1/2 tsp	salt	2 mL
4 tsp	instant espresso powder or coffee granules	20 mL
2 tsp	vanilla	10 mL
3 oz	bittersweet chocolate, grated	90 g

● In bowl, sift flour with 3/4 cup (175 mL) of the sugar; sift again into separate bowl. Set aside.

● In large bowl, beat egg whites until foamy. Add lemon juice, cream of tartar and salt; beat until soft peaks form. Beat in remaining sugar, 2 tbsp (25 mL) at a time, beating until stiff glossy peaks form. Sift flour mixture over top, one-quarter at a time, gently folding in each addition until blended.

● Stir espresso powder with vanilla; fold into batter. Gently fold in chocolate until evenly distributed.

● Scrape into ungreased 10-inch (4 L) tube pan. Run spatula through batter to eliminate any large air pockets; smooth top. Bake in center of 350°F (180°C) oven for 40 to 45 minutes or until cake springs back when lightly touched.

● Turn pan upside down and let hang on legs attached to pan or on inverted funnel or bottle until completely cool. Run thin paring knife around edge of cake to unmould from pan. *(Cake can be stored in airtight container for up to 1 day or wrapped in plastic wrap or foil and frozen in rigid airtight container for up to 1 month.)* Makes 12 servings.

*F*lecks of espresso powder and grated chocolate dress up an airy angel cake and bring it into the coffee-loving nineties.

Per serving: about
- 190 calories
- 5 g protein
- 3 g fat
- 38 g carbohydrate

Chocolate Pound Cake

1 cup	butter, softened	250 mL
2-1/2 cups	granulated sugar	625 mL
3	eggs	3
2 tsp	vanilla	10 mL
2-3/4 cups	all-purpose flour	675 mL
1 cup	unsweetened cocoa powder	250 mL
1 tbsp	baking powder	15 mL
1 tsp	salt	5 mL
1-3/4 cups	milk	425 mL

● In bowl, beat butter with sugar until light and fluffy. Beat in eggs, one at a time, beating well after each addition. Blend in vanilla.

● In separate bowl, stir together flour, cocoa, baking powder and salt. Add to butter mixture alternately with milk, making three additions of flour mixture and two of milk and beating well after each addition. Beat for 2 minutes at medium speed.

● Scrape into greased and floured 10-inch (3 L) Bundt pan. Bake in center of 325°F (160°C) oven for 1-1/2 hours or until cake tester inserted in center comes out clean. Let cool in pan for 10 minutes; turn out onto rack and let cool completely. Makes 16 servings.

*T*he Bundt shape adds a special-occasion feel to any cake, especially this winner in the dark and dense category. Dust with icing sugar, and cut into slices to serve with tea. Or create a restaurant-style dessert by topping a slice with berries, sliced oranges or bananas, a dollop of whipped cream and a drizzle of chocolate sauce.

Per serving: about
- 350 calories
- 5 g protein
- 15 g fat
- 52 g carbohydrate

Chocolate Facts

Glorious chocolate gets its start as beans extracted from the pods of cacao trees grown mainly in equatorial Africa and Central and South America. After harvesting, the beans are fermented in warm, moist conditions for several days, then dried and roasted. The next step is to crack the beans, then winnow them to blow away the shells. What's left is the valuable meat of the beans — the nibs. However, the road to chocolate is far from finished. These nibs are ground into a thick paste that becomes a fluid under the combined effect of heat and grinding; the fluid is known technically as chocolate liquor. More than half of chocolate liquor is a natural vegetable fat called cocoa butter, which has a distinctive melting quality that gives chocolate its seductively unique texture.

Types

The various types of chocolate depend on the proportions of chocolate liquor, cocoa butter and other ingredients, such as sugar. *Canadian Living*'s recipes have been developed for maximum flavor, so do not make substitutions, and do not substitute chocolate chips for chocolate.

● **Bittersweet and semisweet chocolate:** In baking, these types of chocolate are interchangeable, although the bittersweet has a more pronounced chocolate flavor due to its slightly lower sugar content. The formulas for both include pure chocolate liquor (at least 35 percent), with the addition of cocoa butter, sugar, vanilla (which brings out the chocolate flavor) and lecithin, an emulsifier. These chocolates are nice for nibbling, especially if they are of high quality.

● **Sweet chocolate:** This type contains the same ingredients as semisweet, but the proportions are different: less chocolate liquor (a minimum of 15 percent) and more sugar. It's a bit too sweet for nibbling.

● **Unsweetened chocolate:** Also called baking chocolate, unsweetened chocolate is pure chocolate liquor cooled and moulded into blocks. Unsweetened chocolate is just that — not sweetened with sugar and too bitter for nibbling. Don't confuse it with bittersweet chocolate, or with Baker's chocolate, which is a brand name.

● **Milk chocolate:** This type contains the same ingredients as semisweet, bittersweet and sweet chocolate but in a slightly different balance and with the addition of dry or concentrated milk. There must be a minimum of 10 percent chocolate liquor. This chocolate is very susceptible to scorching and should be melted very slowly over hot water (see p. 57). With the exception of milk chocolate chips, do not use milk chocolate as a substitute for other types of chocolate. Milk chocolate is a popular eating chocolate.

● **White chocolate:** This type does not actually contain any chocolate liquor, just cocoa butter, so technically it's not chocolate. The rest of the ingredient list is sugar, dry milk solids and vanilla. Good-quality white chocolate is never pure white but rather ivory or cream-color. Like milk chocolate, white chocolate does not tolerate high heat and, except for white chocolate chips, is not usually used in baking. When buying white chocolate, always check the label. Often the cocoa butter has been replaced in part or completely by other vegetable fats, and this product is called white confectionery coating bars. While it is cheaper than white chocolate, its taste is a pale imitation.

● **Cocoa:** This is made from chocolate liquor that has been pressed to remove most of the cocoa butter, leaving behind a cakelike mass. This mass is first crushed, then pulverized to a powder and sieved. It has a particularly strong flavor, which makes it ideal for cakes and low-fat chocolate desserts. Do not replace this unsweetened cocoa powder with sweetened cocoa powders or hot-chocolate powders.

● The confusion about cocoa powders centers around the distinction between natural (or nonalkalinized) cocoa powder and Dutch-process cocoa; the latter has been treated with an alkaline solution to make the cocoa darker and redder in color and mellower in flavor. Recipes that call for Dutch-process cocoa generally require baking soda as their main leavener. Natural or nonalkalinized cocoa powder is lighter in color, with a robust, slightly sharp flavor. While both kinds of cocoa powders will work in most recipes, it is wise to respect preferences when noted.

TIP: To ensure freshness, purchase chocolate at a store that has a high turnover — and we recommend you buy brand-name chocolate, the best you can afford.

Cheesecake Brownie Cupcakes

1/2 cup	butter, softened	125 mL
1 cup	granulated sugar	250 mL
2	eggs	2
1 tsp	vanilla	5 mL
1/2 cup	sifted unsweetened cocoa powder	125 mL
1/2 cup	all-purpose flour	125 mL
1/4 tsp	salt	1 mL
1	egg yolk	1
1	pkg (125 g) cream cheese, softened	1

● In large bowl, beat butter with 3/4 cup (175 mL) of the sugar until light and fluffy. Beat in eggs, one at a time, beating well after each addition. Beat in vanilla. Stir together cocoa, flour and salt; stir into butter mixture, one-half at a time. Spoon into 12 greased or paper-lined muffin cups.

● In small bowl, beat together remaining sugar, egg yolk and cream cheese; spoon over chocolate mixture. With knife, pull some of the chocolate mixture into cream cheese mixture. Bake in center of 325°F (160°C) oven for 30 minutes or until cake tester inserted in center comes out clean. Let cool in pan on rack. *(Cupcakes can be stored in airtight container for up to 3 days.)* Makes 12 cupcakes.

You can dust the top of these party cupcakes with icing sugar, or finish them off with a swirl of Best-Ever Chocolate Icing (p. 24).

Per cupcake: about
- 220 calories
- 14 g fat
- 3 g protein
- 23 g carbohydrate

TIP: Since there's no messy last-minute cutting, cupcakes are ideal for bake sales, class parties or potluck suppers.

Chocolate Banana Cupcakes ▼

1-2/3 cups	all-purpose flour	400 mL
1/4 cup	unsweetened cocoa powder	50 mL
1 tsp	baking soda	5 mL
1/2 tsp	salt	2 mL
3/4 cup	packed brown sugar	175 mL
3/4 cup	mashed ripe bananas (2 small)	175 mL
3/4 cup	buttermilk	175 mL
1/4 cup	corn syrup	50 mL
3 tbsp	vegetable oil	50 mL
2 tsp	vanilla	10 mL
1/2 cup	chocolate chips	125 mL
	Icing sugar	

● In bowl, mix together flour, cocoa, baking soda and salt. In separate bowl, mix together brown sugar and bananas; stir in buttermilk, corn syrup, oil and vanilla. Pour over flour mixture; stir just until moistened.

● Spoon into 12 greased or paper-lined muffin cups, filling two-thirds full. Sprinkle with chocolate chips. Bake in center of 400°F (200°C) oven for 15 to 20 minutes or until cake tester inserted in center comes out clean. Let cool in pan on rack. Dust with icing sugar. Makes 12 cupcakes.

A few chocolate chips go a long way when they're sprinkled on top of the cupcakes and baked into spiky, melt-in-your-mouth morsels.

Per cupcake: about
- 230 calories
- 7 g fat
- 3 g protein
- 41 g carbohydrate

Pies and Tarts

The velvety smoothness of white and dark chocolate is especially delectable when cupped in a crisp, flaky crust. Match with a touch of fruit, coffee, ginger or nuts for the sheer pleasure of pies and tarts. For the pastry-shy cook, our crusts come in many versions — from an easy-to-handle homemade pastry to phyllo and no-fail cookie crumbs.

White Chocolate Lemon Tart ▶

White chocolate is too sweet for some tastes unless cut with a tangy fruit such as cranberries, orange or lemon. This recipe, which is based on lemon curd, is adapted from a cooking class taken with American master pastry chef Jim Dodge.

Per serving: about
- 510 calories
- 6 g protein
- 33 g fat
- 49 g carbohydrate

TIP: The lemon-curd cream mixture can also be served as a mousse spooned over fresh berries in long-stemmed glasses.

2	eggs	2
2	egg yolks	2
2/3 cup	granulated sugar	150 mL
2 tsp	grated lemon rind	10 mL
1/2 cup	lemon juice	125 mL
3 oz	white chocolate, chopped	90 g
2/3 cup	whipping cream	150 mL
	PASTRY	
1-1/2 cups	all-purpose flour	375 mL
1 tbsp	icing sugar	15 mL
4 tsp	cornstarch	20 mL
3/4 cup	cold butter	175 mL
1 tbsp	white vinegar	15 mL
2 oz	semisweet chocolate, chopped	60 g

● In bowl or top of double boiler over hot (not boiling) water, whisk together eggs, egg yolks, sugar and lemon rind and juice; cook, whisking frequently, for 10 minutes or until translucent and thickened to consistency of pudding. Remove from heat; add white chocolate, stirring until melted. Pour into clean bowl or airtight container; place plastic wrap directly on surface and refrigerate for 1 hour or until chilled. (Lemon curd can be covered and refrigerated for up to 3 days.)

● PASTRY: In large bowl, stir together flour, icing sugar and cornstarch. With pastry blender or two knives, cut in butter until mixture resembles fine crumbs with a few larger pieces. With fork, lightly stir in vinegar until mixture is moistened; let stand for 20 minutes.

● With floured hands, squeeze together small handfuls of dough just until mixture holds together. Press evenly into 1/4-inch (5 mm) thick layer on bottom and up side of 9-inch (23 cm) tart pan with removable bottom. Cover and refrigerate for at least 1 hour or until chilled. (Pastry can be refrigerated for up to 3 days.)

● Prick bottom of pastry shell all over with fork; bake in center of 350°F (180°C) oven for 35 to 40 minutes or until golden. Let cool on rack.

● In bowl over saucepan of hot (not boiling) water, melt semisweet chocolate, stirring occasionally. Using pastry brush, coat inside of pastry shell with chocolate. Let cool.

● In separate bowl, whip cream; using rubber spatula, fold half into lemon curd. Fold in remaining whipped cream just until combined. Pour into shell, swirling top. Refrigerate for 1 hour or until set. (Lemon tart can be covered and refrigerated for up to 24 hours.) Makes 8 servings.

Very Berry Chiffon Pie ◄

35	chocolate wafer cookies (three-quarters of 200 g package)	35
1/4 cup	butter, melted	50 mL
3 oz	bittersweet chocolate, chopped	90 g
	FILLING	
2/3 cup	plain yogurt	150 mL
5 cups	strawberries	1.25 L
3/4 cup	granulated sugar	175 mL
1-1/2 cups	raspberries	375 mL
1/4 cup	lemon juice	50 mL
2 tbsp	orange juice	25 mL
2 tsp	unflavored gelatin	10 mL
2/3 cup	whipping cream	150 mL
	TOPPING	
3 oz	bittersweet chocolate, melted	90 g

● FILLING: Line sieve with double thickness of cheesecloth; set over bowl. Spoon in yogurt; cover and refrigerate to drain for at least 2 hours or for up to 8 hours or until yogurt measures 1/3 cup (75 mL). Discard drained liquid.

● Meanwhile, in food processor, grind cookies to make fine crumbs. Add butter and 1 tbsp (15 mL) water; blend until moistened. Press onto bottom and up side of 9-inch (23 cm) tart pan with removable bottom. Bake in center of 350°F (180°C) oven for 10 minutes or until set. Let cool on rack.

● Meanwhile, in bowl over saucepan of hot (not boiling) water, melt chocolate, stirring occasionally. With spatula, spread gently over pie shell without disturbing crumbs.

● Set aside 10 of the strawberries with hulls. Hull and cut remaining strawberries into quarters, or sixths if large. In food processor, purée together sugar and 1/2 cup (125 mL) each of the strawberries and raspberries. Press through fine sieve into bowl to remove seeds. Stir in remaining raspberries and quartered strawberries; set aside.

● In saucepan, stir lemon juice with orange juice. Sprinkle gelatin over top; let stand for 5 minutes to soften. Warm over low heat, stirring, until liquefied and clear. Stir into berry mixture. Cover and refrigerate for 20 to 30 minutes or until partially set.

● In separate bowl, whip cream. Fold drained yogurt into berry mixture; fold in whipped cream. Spoon into pie shell. Cover loosely with plastic wrap; refrigerate for at least 2 hours or until set or for up to 1 day.

● TOPPING: Dip tip of each reserved strawberry into chocolate; let stand on waxed paper-lined plate until set. With fork, drizzle any remaining chocolate over pie. Arrange strawberries around edge. Makes 10 servings.

VARIATION
● RASPBERRY BLACKBERRY CHIFFON PIE: Increase raspberries to 2-1/2 cups (625 mL). Substitute 1-1/2 cups (375 mL) blackberries, coarsely chopped, for the strawberries. Increase sugar to 1 cup (250 mL). Increase setting time to 4 hours.
For Topping: Reduce chocolate to 1 oz (30 g); drizzle all of it over tart. Garnish with 1/2 cup (125 mL) more raspberries.

There are a lot of berry chiffon pies around, but none as delectable as this one with a chocolate-coated crumb crust and chunks of fresh berries in the creamy filling.

Per serving: about
- 350 calories
- 20 g fat
- high source of iron
- 5 g protein
- 44 g carbohydrate

Tarte au Chocolat

In Montreal, the Pâtisserie de Gascogne serves superb pastries, none better than this reputation-making French-style tart decorated with candied hazelnuts.

Per serving: about
- 495 calories
- 5 g protein
- 36 g fat
- 44 g carbohydrate
- good source of iron

1/3 cup	icing sugar	75 mL
1/2 cup	unsalted butter, softened	125 mL
2 tsp	white vinegar	10 mL
1	egg yolk	1
3/4 cup	ground almonds	175 mL
1-1/3 cups	cake-and-pastry flour	325 mL
Pinch	salt	Pinch
	FILLING	
10 oz	semisweet chocolate, chopped	300 g
1-1/4 cups	whipping cream	300 mL
	TOPPING	
16	whole hazelnuts	16
1/2 cup	granulated sugar	125 mL

● In bowl, beat icing sugar with butter until smooth. Beat together vinegar and egg yolk; beat into butter mixture. Stir in almonds. Stir in flour and salt to make soft dough. Let stand for 10 minutes.

● On lightly floured surface, roll out dough to 1/4-inch (5 mm) thickness. Fit into 9-inch (23 cm) tart pan with removable bottom.

Trim, using extra dough to patch any tears in pastry. Refrigerate for 30 minutes. Prick bottom of pastry shell all over with fork; bake in center of 425°F (220°C) oven for 12 to 15 minutes or until golden brown. Let cool on rack.

● FILLING: Place chocolate in bowl. In saucepan, heat half of the cream over medium heat just until boiling; pour over chocolate, stirring until melted and smooth. Blend in remaining cream. Pour into pastry shell; refrigerate for 1 hour or until set.

● TOPPING: Toast hazelnuts on baking sheet in center of 350°F (180°C) oven for about 8 minutes or until fragrant. Place in tea towel; rub off most of the skins. Set aside.

● In small heavy saucepan, cook sugar over medium-high heat until melted and golden brown. Immediately plunge bottom of pan into cold water for 15 seconds. Working quickly, dip two of the hazelnuts into sugar and place on foil-lined baking sheet. Repeat with remaining hazelnuts. Let cool. Arrange nuts around edge of pie. Makes 10 servings.

Fudge Truffle Tart ▶

Elegant and voluptuous but simple to make, this showstopping dessert tart filled with two-tone ribbons of silky chocolate merits your best serving plate. The tart freezes well; it's also a delight served semifreddo, while still partially frozen.

Per serving: about
- 465 calories
- 5 g protein
- 37 g fat
- 34 g carbohydrate
- good source of iron

2 cups	chocolate wafer cookie crumbs	500 mL
1/3 cup	butter, melted	75 mL
	FILLING	
1 tbsp	instant coffee granules	15 mL
1/4 cup	hot water	50 mL
8 oz	bittersweet chocolate, chopped	250 g
3/4 cup	granulated sugar	175 mL
2/3 cup	butter, cubed	150 mL
6	egg yolks	6
3/4 cup	whipping cream	175 mL
	TOPPING	
1/2 cup	whipping cream	125 mL

● In bowl, stir cookie crumbs with butter until thoroughly moistened. Press onto bottom and up side of 9-inch (23 cm) round tart pan with removable bottom (or 9- x 8-inch/23 x 20 cm rectangular tart pan with removable bottom). Bake in center of 350°F (180°C) oven for 10 minutes or until set. Let cool on rack.

● FILLING: Meanwhile, dissolve coffee granules in hot water. In heavy saucepan, melt chocolate over very low heat; add sugar, butter and coffee, whisking until smooth.

Whisk in egg yolks; cook, whisking constantly, for about 3 minutes or until thickened. Scrape into bowl. Cover with plastic wrap; refrigerate for about 1 hour or until cooled and thickened but still spreadable.

● Spread half of the chocolate mixture over crust. Whip cream. Fold one-third into remaining chocolate mixture; fold in remaining whipped cream. Spread over dark chocolate layer, smoothing and swirling top. Cover and refrigerate for at least 4 hours or until set. Transfer to serving platter. *(Tart can be frozen, then wrapped in plastic wrap and stored in rigid airtight container for up to 1 week; thaw in refrigerator for 15 minutes.)*

● TOPPING: Whip cream; spoon into pastry bag fitted with small rosette tip. Pipe rosettes around border. Makes 12 servings.

TIP: If you don't have chocolate wafer cookie crumbs, you can substitute 1 package (200 g) chocolate cookies, crushed.

STORING CHOCOLATE

● Wrap, then overwrap, chocolate to prevent moisture and odor absorption. Store in cool, dry place for up to six months.

● If you've had chocolate on hand for a while and it has developed a grey or white film, don't be alarmed. This slight discoloration, called "bloom," results from exposure to moisture or extreme changes in temperature. Once chocolate is melted, the discoloration will disappear.

● Frozen chocolate should always be thawed completely without unwrapping in order to prevent moisture from developing on the surface.

Strawberry White Chocolate Tart ◄

3	sheets phyllo pastry	3
3 tbsp	butter, melted	50 mL
3 oz	white chocolate, chopped	90 g
3 cups	strawberries, hulled	750 mL
1 cup	mascarpone cheese (or 8 oz/250 g cream cheese, softened)	250 mL
1/4 cup	18% cream	50 mL
4 tsp	granulated sugar	20 mL
1/2 tsp	vanilla	2 mL

● Cut each sheet of phyllo in half lengthwise to make two 17- x 6-inch (43 x 15 cm) sheets. Lay one piece on work surface, keeping remainder covered with plastic wrap and damp towel. Brush lightly with butter; top with another piece so edges are not perfectly aligned and all eight corners are visible. Repeat with remaining phyllo.

● Gently fit into 14- x 4-inch (35 x 10 cm) tart pan with removable bottom. Turn edges under and ruffle, allowing some to hang over edge. Line with foil; fill with pie weights or dried beans. Bake in center of 375°F (190°C) oven for 10 minutes; remove weights and foil. Prick shell all over with fork; bake for 5 minutes or until golden. Let cool on rack. Remove from pan and place on serving platter.

● In bowl over saucepan of hot (not boiling) water, melt chocolate, stirring occasionally. Spread about two-thirds over crust.

● Slice 1 cup (250 mL) of the strawberries; arrange over chocolate. Beat together mascarpone, cream, sugar and vanilla; spread over strawberries. Halve remaining strawberries; arrange, cut side down, over filling. Drizzle with remaining chocolate. Makes 8 servings.

Juicy red berries, a crisp phyllo shell and a creamy filling make an irresistible combination of textures, tastes and colors.

Per serving: about
- 265 calories
- 4 g protein
- 20 g fat
- 18 g carbohydrate

Chocolate Pumpkin Pie

1	can (14 oz/398 mL) pumpkin purée	1
2/3 cup	packed brown sugar	150 mL
1 tsp	each cinnamon and ginger	5 mL
1/2 tsp	each nutmeg and salt	2 mL
2	eggs, lightly beaten	2
1-2/3 cups	whipping cream	400 mL
3 oz	semisweet chocolate, chopped	90 g
1	unbaked 9-inch (23 cm) deep-dish single-crust pie shell	1
	TOPPING	
1 cup	whipping cream	250 mL
1/2 tsp	granulated sugar	2 mL
1/2 tsp	vanilla	2 mL
1/2 cup	pecan halves, toasted	125 mL

● In large bowl, whisk together pumpkin, brown sugar, cinnamon, ginger, nutmeg and salt; whisk in eggs. In small saucepan, heat cream over medium heat just until bubbles start to form around edge; whisk into pumpkin mixture. Set aside.

● In bowl over saucepan of hot (not boiling) water, melt chocolate, stirring occasionally. Spread over bottom of unbaked pie shell. Place in freezer for about 5 minutes or until firm; pour in pumpkin filling.

● Bake in bottom third of 400°F (200°C) oven for about 50 minutes or until cake tester inserted in center comes out clean. Let cool on rack. Refrigerate for at least 2 hours or for up to 1 day.

● TOPPING: In bowl, whip together cream, sugar and vanilla; spread over pie. Arrange pecans around edge. Makes 8 to 10 servings.

Janet Palmer, innovative Saskatoon baker and owner of the popular Calories restaurant, created this premier pumpkin pie featuring a little twist of ginger and a layer of chocolate in the filling.

Per each of 10 servings: about
- 490 calories
- 5 g protein
- 38 g fat
- 36 g carbohydrate
- good source of iron

TIP: Toast pecans on baking sheet in center of 350°F (180°C) oven for 5 to 10 minutes or just until fragrant; let cool.

Coffee Parfait Pie ▶

No matter how quick and fuss-free ice cream pies are to make, they always rate raves.

Per serving: about
- 330 calories
- 24 g fat
- 5 g protein
- 27 g carbohydrate

TIP: Don't use low-fat ice cream for frozen ice-cream pies since the process of softening them to mould into the crust makes them too hard when refrozen.

1-1/3 cups	chocolate or vanilla wafer cookie crumbs	325 mL
1/3 cup	butter, melted	75 mL
3/4 cup	slivered almonds	175 mL
4 cups	coffee ice cream	1 L
2 tbsp	almond liqueur (optional)	25 mL
1 oz	semisweet chocolate	30 g

● In bowl, stir cookie crumbs with butter until thoroughly moistened. Press onto bottom and up side of 9-inch (23 cm) pie plate. Refrigerate until firm.

● Meanwhile, toast almonds on baking sheet in center of 350°F (180°C) oven for 3 to 5 minutes or until fragrant. Let cool.

● Place ice cream in large chilled bowl; break up into chunks. Using mixer, beat until softened. Add liqueur (if using); beat until blended. Stir in toasted almonds. Spread over crust.

● Using vegetable peeler, shave chocolate over top. Freeze for at least 4 hours or until solid. *(Pie can be wrapped in plastic wrap or foil and stored in rigid airtight container in freezer for up to 1 month.)*

● To serve, remove from freezer and cut immediately into servings using sharp knife; let stand for 5 to 10 minutes. Makes 10 servings.

Best-Ever Chocolate Cream Pie

This is the ultimate chocolate cream pie — a silky smooth and creamy chocolate filling in a crunchy cookie-crumb crust.

Per serving: about
- 410 calories
- 28 g fat
- 6 g protein
- 37 g carbohydrate

2 cups	milk	500 mL
1 cup	18% cream	250 mL
1/2 cup	granulated sugar	125 mL
2	eggs	2
1/4 cup	cornstarch	50 mL
6 oz	semisweet chocolate, chopped	175 g
2 tbsp	unsalted butter	25 mL
2 tsp	vanilla	10 mL
	CRUST	
1-1/3 cups	chocolate wafer cookie crumbs	325 mL
1/4 cup	butter, melted	50 mL
	TOPPING	
3/4 cup	whipping cream	175 mL

● CRUST: In bowl, stir cookie crumbs with butter until moistened. Press onto bottom and up side of 9-inch (23 cm) pie plate. Bake in center of 325°F (160°C) oven for 10 minutes or until set. Let cool on rack.

● In heavy saucepan, heat 1-1/2 cups (375 mL) of the milk and cream over medium heat for about 10 minutes or until bubbles form around edge. In large bowl, whisk together remaining milk, sugar, eggs and cornstarch; whisk in hot milk mixture in slow steady stream, whisking constantly.

● Return warmed egg mixture to pan and bring to boil over medium-high heat, whisking constantly; boil, stirring constantly with wooden spoon, for about 2 minutes or until thickened. Remove from heat.

● Add chocolate, butter and vanilla; whisk until chocolate is melted. Using fine sieve, strain into large bowl. Place plastic wrap directly on surface; refrigerate for about 30 minutes or until cooled to room temperature. Pour into pie shell. Cover loosely and refrigerate for at least 6 hours or for up to 1 day.

● TOPPING: In bowl, whip cream; spread over pie, swirling attractively. Makes 10 servings.

Chocolate Walnut Butter Tart Pie ▼

This chocolate version of an all-Canadian favorite delivers the crunch of walnuts both in the crust and in the filling.

Per each of 12 servings: about
- 535 calories
- 7 g protein
- 32 g fat
- 60 g carbohydrate
- good source of iron

TIP: Use only California walnuts. If they are unavailable, choose pecans instead, since other walnuts are often rancid.

1-1/3 cups	all-purpose flour	325 mL
1/3 cup	ground walnuts	75 mL
2 tbsp	granulated sugar	25 mL
1/4 tsp	salt	1 mL
1/2 cup	butter	125 mL
1/4 cup	shortening	50 mL
1	egg yolk	1
2 tbsp	water	25 mL
2 oz	semisweet chocolate, chopped	60 g
	FILLING	
4	eggs	4
1 cup	granulated sugar	250 mL
1 cup	corn syrup	250 mL
2 tbsp	butter, softened	25 mL
2 tsp	vanilla or coffee liqueur	10 mL
3 oz	semisweet chocolate, chopped	90 g
1-1/2 cups	coarsely chopped walnuts	375 mL

● In large bowl, combine flour, walnuts, sugar and salt. With pastry blender or two knives, cut in butter and shortening until mixture resembles fine crumbs with a few larger pieces.

● Combine egg yolk and water; drizzle over dry ingredients, tossing lightly with fork. Press into disc; wrap and refrigerate for 1 hour.

● On pastry cloth and using stockinette-covered rolling pin, or between two sheets of waxed paper, roll out pastry to 1/4-inch (5 mm) thickness. Ease into 11-inch (28 cm) tart pan with removable bottom; trim excess pastry. Refrigerate for 30 minutes.

● FILLING: In large bowl, beat together eggs, sugar, corn syrup, butter and vanilla; stir in chocolate and walnuts. Spoon into tart shell.

● Bake in center of 375°F (190°C) oven for about 45 minutes or until pastry is browned and tester inserted in center of filling comes out clean. Let cool on rack.

● In bowl over saucepan of hot (not boiling) water, melt chocolate, stirring occasionally. Drizzle over tart. Makes 10 to 12 servings.

Chocolate Almond Fruit Strudel

6	sheets phyllo pastry	6
1/4 cup	unsalted butter, melted	50 mL
1-1/2 tsp	granulated sugar	7 mL
1 tbsp	icing sugar	15 mL
	FILLING	
4 oz	bittersweet chocolate, chopped	125 g
1/3 cup	unsalted butter	75 mL
1 cup	ground almonds	250 mL
3/4 cup	chopped pitted dates	175 mL
3/4 cup	golden raisins	175 mL
1/3 cup	chopped almonds, toasted	75 mL
1/3 cup	chopped figs	75 mL
1/4 cup	icing sugar	50 mL
1 tbsp	coarsely grated orange rind	15 mL
2 tsp	vanilla	10 mL

● FILLING: In bowl over saucepan of hot (not boiling) water, melt chocolate with butter, stirring occasionally. Remove from heat.

Stir in ground almonds, dates, raisins, chopped almonds, figs, sugar, orange rind and vanilla; let cool until as firm as paste.

● Lay one sheet of phyllo on work surface, keeping remainder covered with plastic wrap and damp towel. Brush lightly with butter; sprinkle with 1/2 tsp (2 mL) of the granulated sugar. Top with second sheet of phyllo; brush lightly with butter.

● Scoop out one-third of the filling and press into narrow log; place along long side of phyllo, leaving 1/2 inch (1 cm) of phyllo uncovered at each end. Roll up firmly jelly roll-style; place on large parchment paper-lined baking sheet; brush lightly with butter. Repeat with remaining ingredients to make three rolls.

● Bake in center of 350°F (180°C) oven for about 30 minutes or until golden brown and crisp. Let cool on sheet on rack. Cut into 3/4-inch (2 cm) thick slices. Using sieve, dust with icing sugar. Makes 36 pieces.

Here's a totally new strudel filling — melty chocolate and a tumble of intensely fruity figs, dates, raisins and almonds baked in a log shape and cut neatly into generous bite-size pieces for special sweet trays.

Per piece: about
- 105 calories
- 2 g protein
- 6 g fat
- 12 g carbohydrate

Chocolate Ginger Tassies

1/3 cup	butter, softened	75 mL
1/4 cup	icing sugar, sifted	50 mL
1	egg yolk	1
1/2 tsp	vanilla	2 mL
1 cup	all-purpose flour	250 mL
1 tbsp	cornstarch	15 mL
Pinch	salt	Pinch
	FILLING	
1/4 cup	finely chopped drained preserved ginger	50 mL
1/2 cup	granulated sugar	125 mL
1/4 cup	whipping cream	50 mL
2 tbsp	butter	25 mL
4 oz	semisweet chocolate, chopped	125 g

● In bowl, beat butter with sugar until fluffy. Beat in egg yolk and vanilla. Stir together flour, cornstarch and salt; gradually stir into butter mixture to form smooth dough.

● Place rounded teaspoonfuls (5 mL) of dough into each of thirty-six 1-1/4-inch (3 cm) mini tart tins; evenly press over bottom and up sides and make indentation in center. Bake in center of 325°F (160°C) oven for about 18 minutes or until golden. Let cool in pan for 5 minutes; transfer to racks to let cool completely.

● FILLING: Divide ginger evenly among shells. In small saucepan, bring sugar, cream and butter to boil, stirring. Remove from heat. Add chocolate, stirring until melted. Let cool just to room temperature. Spoon about 1 tsp (5 mL) into each shell. Let cool until set. Makes 36 tartlets.

Start off tassies (small cups) with a melt-in-your-mouth, pat-in pastry and fill with preserved ginger — the kind in the jar with syrup — and a dollop of chocolate ganache. Sophisticated, yet very approachable!

Per tartlet: about
- 80 calories
- 1 g protein
- 4 g fat
- 10 g carbohydrate

Chocolate Tartlets

A dark chocolate pastry, quickly whizzed up in the food processor, cups a dollop of Creamy Filling (recipe, this page) and perfect whole berries. Replace strawberries with blueberries or raspberries as the summer advances.

Per shell: about
- 70 calories
- 5 g fat
- 1 g protein
- 7 g carbohydrate

8 oz	semisweet chocolate, chopped	250 g
2 tbsp	water	25 mL
1/2 tsp	vanilla	2 mL
2 cups	all-purpose flour	500 mL
1/2 tsp	salt	2 mL
3/4 cup	cold butter	175 mL

● In bowl over saucepan of hot (not boiling) water, melt chocolate, stirring occasionally; remove from heat. Stir in water and vanilla.

● In food processor or in bowl using pastry blender or two knives, combine flour and salt; cut in butter until crumbly. Add chocolate; mix until soft dough forms. Divide into four balls; flatten, wrap and chill for about 30 minutes or until firm. *(Pastry can be refrigerated for up to 1 week or frozen for up to 2 months.)*

● Let dough soften slightly at room temperature. Between sheets of waxed paper, roll out each portion to 1/8-inch (3 mm) thickness. Lift off top sheet of paper; using floured 2-1/2-inch (6 cm) cutter, cut out rounds. Using spatula, transfer to 2-1/2-inch (6 cm) tart shells or 2-1/4-inch (5 cm) tart tins; press gently to sides. Prick bottom and sides with fork.

● Bake in center of 350°F (180°C) oven for 10 minutes. Prick again on bottom if puffed. Bake for about 5 minutes longer or until slightly firm. Let cool in pans for 2 minutes; transfer to racks and let cool completely. Makes about 48 tartlet shells.

CREAMY FILLING

● In bowl, beat 3/4 cup (175 mL) softened cream cheese with 4 tsp (20 mL) icing sugar; gradually beat in 1/3 cup (75 mL) whipping cream until smooth. Stir in 1/2 tsp (2 mL) vanilla. Chill for at least 30 minutes before using. Makes about 1-1/3 cups (325 mL), enough for 4 dozen tarts or meringues or 1 pie.

Per tsp (5 mL): about • 14 calories • trace protein • 1 g fat • trace carbohydrate

---

TIP: You will need about 4 cups (1 L) medium/small berries to fill 48 tartlet shells.

Chocolate, Nut and Date Baklava ▶

Honey and orange juice drench flaky diamond-shaped pieces of baklava. The chocolate and date filling is a welcome departure from the usual nuts. Since the pastry is very sweet, do as the Greeks do and serve in the afternoon or evening with coffee or tea.

Per serving: about
- 240 calories
- 15 g fat
- 3 g protein
- 28 g carbohydrate

2 cups	coarsely chopped pecans	500 mL
1 cup	chopped dates	250 mL
6 oz	bittersweet chocolate, chopped	175 g
1 tbsp	granulated sugar	15 mL
2 tsp	cinnamon	10 mL
2 tsp	grated orange rind	10 mL
12	sheets phyllo pastry	12
2/3 cup	butter, melted	150 mL

	TOPPING	
3/4 cup	liquid honey	175 mL
1/4 cup	orange juice	50 mL
1 oz	bittersweet chocolate, chopped	30 g

● Toast pecans on baking sheet in center of 350°F (180°C) oven for 5 to 10 minutes or until fragrant; let cool. In bowl, toss together pecans, dates, chocolate, sugar, cinnamon and orange rind. Set aside.

● Place one sheet of phyllo on work surface, keeping remainder covered with plastic wrap and damp towel. Brush lightly with butter. Fold in half crosswise; brush lightly with

butter. Place in greased 13- x 9-inch (3.5 L) cake pan. Repeat with three more sheets of phyllo for a total of eight layers.

● Sprinkle with one-third of the chocolate mixture. Lightly brush two more sheets of phyllo with butter; fold each in half and place over chocolate mixture. Sprinkle with another one-third of the mixture. Brush two more sheets of phyllo with butter; fold each in half and place on top. Sprinkle with remaining chocolate mixture. Brush remaining phyllo with butter; fold each

in half and place in pan. Brush top sheet with remaining butter. Tuck in any excess.

● Using sharp knife and without cutting all the way through to filling, make long diagonal cuts, 1-1/2 inches (4 cm) apart, through top layers of phyllo, first in one direction, then opposite, to form diamond shapes. Bake in center of 350°F (180°C) oven for 40 to 45 minutes or until golden brown and flaky on top.

● TOPPING: Meanwhile, in small saucepan, whisk honey with orange juice; bring to boil over medium-high heat. Reduce heat and simmer for 5 minutes, whisking occasionally. Spoon over hot baklava. Let cool completely on rack. *(Baklava can be covered with plastic wrap and stored at room temperature for up to 1 day.)*

● In bowl over saucepan of hot (not boiling) water, melt chocolate, stirring occasionally. Drizzle over baklava. Cut into diamond shapes. Makes 24 servings.

Spoon Desserts

Some call them puddings, but somehow that word doesn't invite you as temptingly as it should to the delicious variety of these desserts — from airy mousses, show-off soufflés and silky smooth ice creams to dense and luscious pâtés and comfy baked or steamed puddings.

Chocolate Soufflé ▶

An airy puff of gossamer chocolate brought to the table with a flourish — that's a soufflé, and it never fails to win the kind of accolades reserved for a dish that's complicated or requires enormous skill. The truth is, soufflés are utterly do-able!

Per serving: about
- 232 calories
- 5 g protein
- 12 g fat
- 29 g carbohydrate

2 oz	unsweetened chocolate, chopped	60 g
2 tbsp	butter	25 mL
4	eggs, separated	4
2/3 cup	granulated sugar	150 mL
2 tbsp	hazelnut liqueur, rum or strong coffee	25 mL
1/4 tsp	cream of tartar	1 mL
1 tbsp	icing sugar or unsweetened cocoa powder	15 mL
1/2 cup	whipping cream, whipped (optional)	125 mL

● Fold 24-inch (60 cm) long piece of foil in half lengthwise; generously butter 3-inch (8 cm) strip lengthwise along one edge. Wrap around outside of 6- to 7-inch (1.175 to 1.5 L) straight-sided soufflé dish, with buttered strip facing in and extending above rim; secure with string.

● In bowl over saucepan of hot (not boiling) water, melt chocolate with butter, stirring occasionally.

● In separate bowl, beat egg yolks with half of the granulated sugar for about 5 minutes or until thickened and mixture falls in ribbons when beaters are lifted. Add chocolate mixture and liqueur; beat until thoroughly blended.

● In another bowl, beat egg whites with cream of tartar until soft peaks form. Gradually beat in remaining granulated sugar, 2 tbsp (25 mL) at a time, until stiff peaks form.

● Fold one-quarter into chocolate mixture; gently fold in remaining egg whites. Scrape into prepared dish. *(Soufflé can be refrigerated for up to 1 hour before baking.)*

● Place dish on baking sheet. Bake in lower third of 375°F (190°C) oven for about 35 minutes or until puffed and almost firm to the touch. Cut string; remove foil. Dust with icing sugar. Serve immediately. Top with spoonful of whipped cream (if using). Makes 6 servings.

VARIATION
● MINI CHOCOLATE SOUFFLÉS: Use six 3-1/2-inch (150 mL) ramekins instead of soufflé dish; use 12- x 6-inch (30 x 15 cm) piece of foil for each, buttering 2-inch (5 cm) strip. Reduce baking time to about 25 minutes.

Chocolate Fondue with Banana Bread ▼

Got kids? Haul that old chocolate fondue set out of the attic because kids love fondue — it's the fun of dunking, nibbling and chatting. Try fondues after a chilly hike or a day in the snow, or even in the cool of a summer evening.

Per serving (with Banana Bread): about

- 865 calories
- 13 g protein
- 51 g fat
- 105 g carbohydrate
- very high source of fiber
- good source of calcium
- excellent source of iron

	Banana Bread (recipe follows)	
1 cup	fresh pineapple chunks, drained well	250 mL
1 cup	red seedless grapes	250 mL
2	clementines, peeled and sectioned	2
1	pear, cut in chunks	1
	CHOCOLATE FONDUE	
6 oz	bittersweet chocolate, chopped	175 g
4 oz	milk chocolate, chopped	125 g
3/4 cup	whipping cream	175 mL
2 tbsp	amaretto, brandy or rum (optional)	25 mL

● CHOCOLATE FONDUE: Place bittersweet and milk chocolates in fondue pot. In small saucepan, heat cream to boiling; pour over chocolate and stir until melted. Add amaretto (if using). Set over fondue warmer.

● Cut banana bread into four 3/4-inch (2 cm) thick slices; cut each into 6 pieces. Reserve remaining bread for another use. Arrange bread, pineapple, grapes, clementines and pear around fondue pot. To serve, pierce fruit and bread with fondue fork; dip into chocolate. Makes 4 servings.

	BANANA BREAD	
1/2 cup	granulated sugar	125 mL
1/4 cup	vegetable oil	50 mL
2	eggs	2
1 cup	mashed bananas	250 mL
1 tsp	vanilla	5 mL
2 cups	all-purpose flour	500 mL
2 tsp	baking powder	10 mL
1/2 tsp	baking soda	2 mL
1/2 tsp	salt	2 mL
1/2 cup	buttermilk	125 mL

● In bowl, whisk together granulated sugar and oil; whisk in eggs, one at a time, beating well after each addition. Stir in bananas and vanilla.

● Combine flour, baking powder, baking soda and salt; stir into banana mixture alternately with buttermilk, making three additions of flour mixture and two of buttermilk.

● Pour batter into greased 8- x 4-inch (1.5 L) loaf pan. Bake in center of 350°F (180°C) oven for about 1 hour or until cake tester inserted in center comes out clean. Let cool in pan on rack for 15 minutes. Remove from pan and let cool completely on rack. *(Bread can be wrapped in plastic wrap and stored for up to 1 day or frozen in airtight container for up to 2 weeks.)* Makes 12 slices.

Per slice: about • 185 calories • 4 g protein • 6 g fat • 30 g carbohydrate

Chocolate Bread Pudding

1/3 cup	brandy or cherry nectar	75 mL
2/3 cup	dried cherries or raisins	150 mL
12	slices egg bread	12
3 oz	semisweet chocolate, chopped	90 g
3 cups	milk	750 mL
6	eggs	6
1 cup	whipping cream	250 mL
2/3 cup	granulated sugar	150 mL
1/4 cup	sifted unsweetened cocoa powder	50 mL
1 tbsp	instant coffee granules	15 mL
1-1/2 tsp	vanilla	7 mL

● In saucepan, heat brandy just until steaming; stir in cherries. Remove from heat; cover and let stand for 10 minutes.

● Cut each slice of bread into 4 triangles; arrange on baking sheets. Bake in center of 300°F (150°C) oven for 10 minutes or until dried out. Line bottom of greased 10-cup (2.5 L) oval baking dish with single layer of bread triangles. Arrange remaining bread in overlapping layer on top. Reserving brandy, drain cherries. Sprinkle 1/2 cup (125 mL) of the cherries over bread.

● Place chocolate in bowl. In saucepan, heat milk until steaming; pour over chocolate and stir until melted. In large bowl, whisk together eggs, cream, sugar, cocoa and coffee granules; whisk in milk mixture, reserved brandy and vanilla. Pour over bread; let stand for 15 minutes.

● Press bread down with rubber spatula to soak thoroughly; sprinkle with remaining cherries. Place dish in large roasting pan; pour in enough hot water to come halfway up side of baking dish. Bake in center of 325°F (160°C) oven for about 40 minutes or until cake tester inserted in center of pudding comes out clean. Makes 10 to 12 servings.

On a comfort scale, both bread pudding and chocolate are tops. Together, they're bliss on a spoon, especially when served with crème anglaise with a few drops of raspberry coulis.

Per each of 12 servings: about
- 370 calories
- 16 g fat
- good source of iron
- 10 g protein
- 47 g carbohydrate

TIP: You can use a 13- x 9-inch (3 L) glass baking dish instead of the oval dish, if desired.

Chocolate Pudding Cake

1-1/3 cups	milk	325 mL
1/2 cup	granulated sugar	125 mL
1/4 cup	sifted unsweetened cocoa powder	50 mL
1 tbsp	instant coffee granules	15 mL
1 tsp	cornstarch	5 mL
	CAKE	
2 oz	milk chocolate, chopped	60 g
2 tbsp	butter	25 mL
3/4 cup	all-purpose flour	175 mL
1/2 cup	granulated sugar	125 mL
2 tbsp	sifted unsweetened cocoa powder	25 mL
1 tsp	baking powder	5 mL
1	egg	1
1/3 cup	milk	75 mL
1-1/2 tsp	vanilla	7 mL

● In saucepan, whisk together milk, sugar, cocoa, coffee granules and cornstarch over medium heat for 5 minutes or until lukewarm; remove from heat. Cover; set sauce aside.

● CAKE: In bowl over saucepan of hot (not boiling) water, melt milk chocolate with butter, stirring occasionally. Let cool slightly. In large bowl, stir together flour, sugar, cocoa and baking powder. Combine egg, milk, vanilla and chocolate mixture; pour over dry ingredients and stir just until moistened. Pour into greased 8-inch (2 L) square baking dish; spread evenly.

● In slow steady stream, gently pour sauce evenly over cake batter. Bake in center of 350°F (180°C) oven for about 30 minutes or until cake tester inserted in center of cake comes out clean. Let stand for about 10 minutes or until slightly cooled. Serve warm. Makes 6 to 8 servings.

This creamy-custard-on-the-bottom-and-cake-on-the-top pudding goes back decades, but there's nothing old about the way each generation of cooks discovers it with renewed pleasure and enthusiasm.

Per each of 8 servings: about
- 255 calories
- 8 g fat
- 5 g protein
- 43 g carbohydrate

White Chocolate and Raspberry Parfait ▼

This stunning layered white chocolate and raspberry confection will establish your reputation as a top-notch dessert maker.

Per serving: about
- 315 calories
- 3 g protein
- 20 g fat
- 33 g carbohydrate

2	pkg (300 g each) frozen unsweetened raspberries, thawed	2
1-1/4 cups	granulated sugar	300 mL
1 tbsp	kirsch (optional)	15 mL
4 oz	white chocolate, chopped	125 g
6	egg yolks	6
1 tsp	vanilla	5 mL
2 cups	whipping cream	500 mL

● Line 8- x 4-inch (1.5 L) loaf pan with plastic wrap, leaving 2-inch (5 cm) overhang on all sides. Set aside.

● In food processor, purée raspberries. Press through sieve over bowl to remove seeds and extract 2 cups (500 mL) purée. Whisk in 1/2 cup (125 mL) of the sugar, and kirsch (if using). Set aside 1 cup (250 mL) of the purée at room temperature. Cover and refrigerate remaining purée.

● In bowl over saucepan of hot (not boiling) water, melt chocolate, stirring occasionally. Let cool to room temperature.

● In separate bowl over saucepan of simmering water and using electric beater, beat egg yolks with remaining sugar for 7 to 10 minutes or until instant-read thermometer registers 140°F (60°C). Remove from heat. Beat in chocolate and vanilla. Let stand for 15 to 20 minutes or until cooled. Whip cream; fold one-third into chocolate mixture. Fold in remaining whipped cream.

● Fold 1-1/3 cups (325 mL) of the chocolate mixture into reserved room-temperature raspberry purée. Pour half of the remaining chocolate mixture into prepared pan, smoothing surface. Pour in half of the raspberry mixture to evenly cover surface. Repeat layers once. Cover with plastic wrap and freeze for at least 12 hours. *(Parfait can be frozen for up to 3 days.)*

● Uncover pan; holding sideways, run under hot water for 30 to 60 seconds, or let stand at room temperature for 5 minutes. Invert onto platter, tapping gently to remove pan. Peel away plastic wrap; smooth sides. Whisk refrigerated purée. Slice parfait thinly and serve topped with purée. Makes 12 servings.

TIP: This dessert can also be arranged in alternating layers in parfait glasses. If desired, tilt glass while spooning in layers. Prop, tilted, in freezer until set (as in photo). Top with whipped cream or raspberry purée.

Chocolate Steamed Pudding

1-2/3 cups	all-purpose flour	400 mL
1/2 cup	unsweetened cocoa powder	125 mL
1 tsp	baking soda	5 mL
1/2 tsp	salt	2 mL
1/2 tsp	cinnamon	2 mL
3/4 cup	golden raisins	175 mL
3/4 cup	dried apricots, chopped	175 mL
1/2 cup	dried cherries	125 mL
1/2 cup	chocolate chips	125 mL
2/3 cup	packed brown sugar	150 mL
1/2 cup	butter, softened	125 mL
3	eggs	3
1/3 cup	apricot jam	75 mL
1/4 cup	brandy	50 mL
1 tbsp	grated orange rind	15 mL

● Grease 7- or 8-cup (1.75 or 2 L) pudding mould; line bottom with greased waxed paper, pressing into pattern in mould. Set aside.

● In large bowl, stir together flour, cocoa, baking soda, salt and cinnamon; stir in raisins, apricots, cherries and chocolate chips.

● In separate bowl, beat sugar with butter until light and fluffy. Beat in eggs, one at a time. Add apricot jam, brandy and orange rind; beat until smooth. With wooden spoon, stir in flour mixture, 1/2 cup (125 mL) at a time, just until combined.

● Pack batter into prepared mould; place piece of waxed paper directly on surface. Cover mould with lid. (Or make 1-inch/2.5 cm pleat across middle of large piece of foil and fit over top, pressing down sides; trim edge, leaving 2-inch/5 cm overhang. Tie string securely around top of mould; fold foil overhang upward over string.)

● Place mould on rack in large stockpot; pour in enough boiling water to come two-thirds up side of mould. Cover and simmer over medium heat, adding water as needed to maintain level, for about 2 hours or until cake tester inserted in center comes out clean.

● Remove from pot and let stand on rack for 10 minutes. Remove paper and run knife around pudding; unmould onto serving plate. *(Pudding can be wrapped in plastic wrap and refrigerated for up to 2 weeks or frozen in rigid airtight container for up to 3 weeks.)* Makes 8 servings.

Marry a classic steamed fruit pudding with modern dark chocolate for a dessert that intrigues and pleases. Steaming, by the way, is an easy, almost foolproof cooking method.

Per serving: about
- 510 calories
- 19 g fat
- excellent source of iron
- 8 g protein
- 84 g carbohydrate
- high source of fiber

TIP: To resteam pudding, unwrap and return to greased and paper-lined mould. Cover and steam as directed in recipe, reducing time by about 30 minutes.

Chocolate Chestnut Mousse

6 oz	bittersweet chocolate, chopped	175 g
1-1/2 cups	sweetened chestnut purée	375 mL
3 tbsp	dark rum	50 mL
1-1/2 cups	whipping cream	375 mL
3	egg whites	3

● In bowl over saucepan of hot (not boiling) water, melt chocolate, stirring occasionally; let cool slightly.

● In large bowl, stir together chocolate, chestnut purée and rum until blended. In separate bowl, whip cream. Fold one-third into chocolate mixture; fold in remaining whipped cream.

● In separate bowl, beat egg whites until stiff peaks form; fold into chocolate mixture. Spoon into wine glasses or custard cups. Cover and refrigerate for 2 hours or until chilled. *(Mousse can be refrigerated for up to 1 day.)* Makes 8 servings.

Serving dessert in wine glasses adds an extra measure of style.

Per serving: about
- 380 calories
- 24 g fat
- 4 g protein
- 39 g carbohydrate

Chocolate Banana Pudding ▶

This pudding, with all the old-fashioned flavor kids love, is lightened up by using egg whites instead of whole eggs, and cornstarch as thickening.

Per serving: about
- 285 calories
- 8 g protein
- 5 g fat
- 56 g carbohydrate
- good source of calcium

2-1/4 cups	milk	550 mL
2/3 cup	granulated sugar	150 mL
2	egg whites	2
1/3 cup	unsweetened cocoa powder	75 mL
3 tbsp	cornstarch	50 mL
2 tsp	vanilla	10 mL
1	banana	1

● In heavy saucepan, heat 2 cups (500 mL) of the milk with sugar over medium heat, stirring often, for about 5 minutes or just until bubbles form around edge.

● Meanwhile, in bowl, whisk together remaining milk, egg whites, cocoa and cornstarch; gradually whisk in hot milk mixture. Pour into clean saucepan; cook over medium heat, stirring with wooden spoon, for 10 minutes or until consistency of melted chocolate. Let cool slightly; stir in vanilla.

● Place plastic wrap directly on surface; refrigerate for at least 2 hours or until cold. *(Pudding can be prepared to this point and refrigerated for up to 2 days.)* Just before serving, dice banana; stir into pudding. Makes 4 servings.

Chocolate Mousse-Filled Hearts

Does chocolate put you in the mood for romance? Chemicals in chocolate do indeed simulate that feeling of happiness — and when the chocolate is heart-shaped, who can resist?

Per serving: about
- 465 calories
- 5 g protein
- 41 g fat
- 30 g carbohydrate
- good source of iron

4 oz	bittersweet or semisweet chocolate, chopped	125 g
	MOUSSE	
2 oz	bittersweet or semisweet chocolate, chopped	60 g
2/3 cup	whipping cream	150 mL
	GARNISH	
1 oz	white chocolate, melted	30 g

● In bowl over saucepan of hot (not boiling) water, melt bittersweet chocolate, stirring occasionally. Pour onto waxed paper-lined baking sheet; using palette knife or rubber spatula, spread into 14- x 8-inch (35 x 20 cm) rectangle. Refrigerate for 15 minutes or until hardened.

● Let chocolate stand at room temperature for 5 minutes or until no longer brittle. Using 3-1/2-inch (9 cm) heart-shaped cookie cutter, cut eight hearts, alternating tops and bottoms and leaving hearts in place on sheet. Refrigerate for 5 minutes or until hardened.

Using knife, carefully lift out hearts and place on another waxed paper-lined baking sheet. (Scraps can be kept for another use.) Return hearts to refrigerator.

● MOUSSE: Place chocolate in bowl. In saucepan, bring 1/3 cup (75 mL) of the cream just to boil; pour over chocolate, whisking until smooth. Refrigerate for 30 minutes or until slightly thickened and chilled.

● In bowl, whip remaining cream; fold half into chilled chocolate mixture. Fold in remaining whipped cream. Scrape into piping bag fitted with star tip, or use spoon; pipe or spoon onto four of the hearts to cover completely. Top with remaining hearts, dull side down.

● GARNISH: With fork, drizzle white chocolate over hearts. Cover lightly with plastic wrap; refrigerate for at least 1 hour or until slightly hardened. *(Hearts can be refrigerated for up to 24 hours; let stand at room temperature for 10 minutes before serving.)* Makes 4 servings.

Clockwise from left: Chocolate Banana Pudding; Butterscotch Pudding With Chocolate Garnish; (on plate) Cappuccino Cheesecake Squares (p. 75) and Lean But Luscious Brownies (p. 72); Crunchy Oatmeal Chippers (p. 64)

Baked Chocolate Mousse

A whisp of cinnamon adds a Mexican touch to this dense and delicious mousse.

Per serving: about
- 250 calories
- 3 g protein
- 19 g fat
- 21 g carbohydrate

1/2 cup	granulated sugar	125 mL
1/3 cup	butter, in pieces	75 mL
12 oz	semisweet chocolate, chopped	375 g
4	eggs	4
2	egg yolks	2
2 tbsp	instant coffee granules	25 mL
1/2 tsp	cinnamon	2 mL
	GARNISH	
1 cup	whipping cream	250 mL
2 tbsp	granulated sugar	25 mL
1 tsp	cinnamon	5 mL
1/2 tsp	unsweetened cocoa powder	2 mL

● Line bottom of 8-inch (1.2 L) round cake pan with parchment or waxed paper. Set aside.

● In saucepan, stir sugar with 1/3 cup (75 mL) water over medium heat until dissolved. Add butter; simmer, stirring occasionally, until melted and about to boil. Remove from heat. Add chocolate; whisk until melted.

● In bowl, whisk eggs with egg yolks; whisk into chocolate mixture in two additions. Dissolve coffee granules in 1/3 cup (75 mL) warm water; whisk into chocolate mixture along with cinnamon.

● Scrape into prepared pan. Set pan in larger pan; pour in enough hot water to come halfway up side of cake pan. Bake in center of 325°F (160°C) oven for 35 to 40 minutes or just until firm to the touch at edge but still slightly jiggly in center. Remove from water; let cool completely on rack. *(Mousse can be wrapped in plastic wrap and refrigerated for up to 5 days or frozen in rigid airtight container for up to 1 month; thaw in refrigerator for 8 hours.)*

● Run thin knife around mousse to loosen from pan; invert onto cake plate, shaking pan slightly. Peel off paper.

● GARNISH: In bowl, whip cream with sugar; mound on top of mousse. Combine cinnamon with cocoa; sprinkle over top. Makes 16 servings.

Truffle Pots de Crème

*S*erved warm, these little pots of indulgence are silky and soft. Chilled, they firm up into adult versions of Fudgsicles.

Per serving: about
- 435 calories
- 6 g protein
- 37 g fat
- 26 g carbohydrate

6 oz	bittersweet chocolate, chopped	175 g
1-1/2 cups	whipping cream	375 mL
6	egg yolks	6
1/3 cup	granulated sugar	75 mL
1 tbsp	brandy (optional)	15 mL
Dash	vanilla	Dash

● Place chocolate in bowl. In saucepan, bring cream just to boil; pour one-third over chocolate, whisking until melted. Gradually stir in remaining cream.

● In separate bowl, whisk egg yolks with sugar until well combined. Whisk in one-third of the chocolate mixture; stir in remaining chocolate mixture. Stir in brandy (if using) and vanilla.

● Pour into six 3/4-cup (175 mL) custard cups or heatproof ramekins. Place in 13- x 9-inch (3.5 L) cake pan; pour in enough boiling water to come halfway up sides of cups.

● Bake in center of 325°F (160°C) oven for 25 to 30 minutes or until set around edge but still slightly jiggly in center. Remove cups from pan; let cool on rack for at least 30 minutes or for up to 2 hours. Makes 6 servings.

Light Pots de Crème

2/3 cup	granulated sugar	175 mL
1/2 cup	sifted unsweetened cocoa powder	125 mL
2	egg yolks	2
1	egg	1
1	can (385 mL) 2% evaporated milk	1
1/3 cup	strong coffee, cooled	75 mL
2 tbsp	orange liqueur or thawed orange juice concentrate	25 mL
2 oz	white chocolate, chopped	60 g

● In large bowl, combine sugar and cocoa; stir in egg yolks and egg until smooth. Gradually whisk in evaporated milk, coffee and liqueur. Strain mixture; divide evenly among six 3/4-cup (175 mL) custard cups or heatproof ramekins.

● Place custard cups in 13- x 9-inch (3.5 L) cake pan. Pour in enough boiling water to come three-quarters of the way up sides of cups; cover pan with foil. Bake in center of 325°F (160°C) oven for 45 to 50 minutes or until knife inserted at edge comes out clean but center is still jiggly. Remove cups from pan; let cool on racks to room temperature. Refrigerate for at least 1 hour or until chilled. *(Pots de crème can be refrigerated for up to 12 hours.)*

● In small bowl over saucepan of hot (not boiling) water, melt white chocolate, stirring occasionally. Using paper towel, gently blot any moisture from surface of custard. Drizzle chocolate over top. Refrigerate for about 5 minutes or until chocolate is set. Makes 6 servings.

With evaporated milk, you still get all the creaminess you expect in a fancy custard — but with a lot less fat.

Per serving: about
- 270 calories
- 9 g fat
- good source of calcium
- 9 g protein
- 41 g carbohydrate

TIP: For an extra hit of mocha, you can omit the orange liqueur or juice and increase the coffee to 1/2 cup (125 mL).

MELTING CHOCOLATE

The key word is patience, and that means low heat, and time. Chop chocolate to expose as much surface area as possible.

● **Stove top:** Place chopped chocolate in dry heatproof glass or stainless steel bowl set over slightly smaller saucepan of hot (not boiling) water or in top of double boiler. If the bowl is too large, it may be heated by the element, causing the chocolate to burn. Make sure the bottom of the bowl does not touch the water. Let about three-quarters of the chocolate melt; remove from heat and stir with a dry metal spoon, letting residual heat melt the remaining chocolate.

Never cover the chocolate because droplets of moisture can accumulate on the cover and drop back into the chocolate, causing it to seize.

● **Microwave:** Melt small amounts of chocolate at Medium (50%) power only, at 30-second intervals and stirring frequently. The inside of the chocolate will melt before the surface even appears warm, and the melting will continue even after the chocolate has been removed from the microwave. Your best bet is to stop

microwaving before the chocolate is fully melted and stir to finish it off. Do not use the microwave to melt white or milk chocolate.

● Chocolate melted alone is most vulnerable and burns easily, even at temperatures your hand can bear, promptly seizing up into a grainy mass. Chocolate melted with a small amount of liquid, such as drops of moisture in a bowl or off a lid or wooden spoon, can also clump and seize up.

● It is almost impossible to reliquefy chocolate that has seized up. You can try immediately stirring in 1 tbsp (15 mL) vegetable oil per 6 oz (175 g) chocolate. If this doesn't work, remove from pot and let harden to use later in another recipe calling for melting the chocolate with liquid.

● Chocolate melts reliably when combined with liquid in a recipe, but there must be enough liquid (at least 1 tbsp/15 mL per 2 oz/60 g chocolate).

Two-Chocolate Crème Brûlée

A lacy crust of bittersweet chocolate, instead of the usual caramelized sugar, films the top of rich chocolate custards.

Per serving: about
- 360 calories
- 4 g protein
- 31 g fat
- 19 g carbohydrate

2 cups	whipping cream	500 mL
1/3 cup	granulated sugar	75 mL
3 oz	white chocolate, chopped	90 g
5	egg yolks	5
1/2 tsp	vanilla	2 mL
2 oz	bittersweet chocolate, chopped	60 g

● In heavy saucepan, stir cream with sugar over medium-low heat until bubbles form around edge. Add white chocolate, whisking until smooth. Remove from heat.

● In large liquid measure, whisk egg yolks with vanilla until smooth; whisk in cream mixture. Strain through fine sieve. Pour into eight 1/3-cup (75 mL) custard cups or heatproof ramekins. Place in large shallow pan; pour in enough boiling water to come halfway up sides of cups.

● Bake in center of 300°F (150°C) oven for about 40 minutes or until tops are firm and custards are set but still creamy. Let cool on rack. Refrigerate for at least 4 hours or until chilled. *(Custards can be loosely covered and refrigerated for up to 2 days.)*

● In bowl over saucepan of hot (not boiling) water, melt bittersweet chocolate, stirring occasionally. Scrape into small sturdy plastic bag. Snip off tiny bit of corner; using brisk back-and-forth motion, drizzle chocolate over custards. Refrigerate for at least 30 minutes or until chocolate is firm. *(Brûlée can be covered with plastic wrap and refrigerated for up to 2 days.)* Makes 8 servings.

VARIATIONS

● BERRY CHOCOLATE CRÈME BRÛLÉE: Top each chilled custard with rounded tablespoonful (15 mL) of raspberries or blueberries. Drizzle with melted bittersweet or white chocolate.

● GINGER CHOCOLATE CRÉME BRÛLÉE: Stir 1/4 cup (50 mL) finely chopped preserved ginger and 2 tbsp (25 mL) ginger syrup into cream before heating. (Be sure to divide ginger evenly among custard cups.)

Chocolate Fudge Sauce

A thick, gooey chocolate sauce is perfect for spooning over ice cream, fruit or whatever else your heart desires.

Per 2 tbsp (25 mL): about
- 125 calories
- 2 g protein
- 7 g fat
- 19 g carbohydrate

1/3 cup	unsweetened cocoa powder	75 mL
1/3 cup	corn syrup	75 mL
4 oz	bittersweet chocolate, chopped	125 g
1 tsp	vanilla	5 mL

● In small saucepan, bring cocoa, 1/2 cup (125 mL) water and corn syrup to boil over medium heat, whisking constantly; boil for 2 minutes.

● Reduce heat to low. Add chocolate; cook, stirring, until melted. Remove from heat; stir in vanilla. Transfer to bowl and cover with plastic wrap. Serve warm or refrigerate until chilled. *(Sauce can be refrigerated in airtight container for up to 2 weeks; reheat in saucepan over low heat or in microwave at Low/10% until pourable.)* Makes 1 cup (250 mL).

Chocolate Pâté

8 oz	unsweetened chocolate, chopped	250 g
1 cup	instant dissolving (fruit/berry) sugar	250 mL
1/2 cup	hot strong coffee	125 mL
1 cup	butter, cubed	250 mL
4	eggs	4
1 tbsp	all-purpose flour	15 mL
2 oz	semisweet chocolate, grated	60 g

● Grease 9- x 5-inch (2 L) loaf pan; line with foil, leaving 2-inch (5 cm) overhang and pressing foil smoothly to bottom and along sides. Set aside.

● In large bowl over saucepan of hot (not boiling) water, melt together unsweetened chocolate, sugar and coffee, stirring occasionally, until smooth. Remove from heat; stir in butter, a little at a time, thoroughly incorporating into chocolate mixture after each addition.

● In separate bowl, beat eggs lightly; gradually whisk in flour. Gently fold into chocolate mixture until well blended. Pour into prepared pan, spreading evenly.

● Set larger roasting or cake pan on stove top and pour in enough water to come 1 inch (2.5 cm) up sides; bring to just below simmer. Place loaf pan in water and simmer for 45 minutes, making sure water does not boil.

● Transfer loaf pan to center of 225°F (110°C) oven; bake for 25 to 30 minutes or until edges are set but center is still slightly jiggly. Transfer to rack; let cool. Cover with clean tea towel and refrigerate for at least 1 day or for up to 2 days.

● Using foil overhang, lift pâté from pan; invert onto serving plate and peel off foil. Sprinkle with grated chocolate. Makes 16 servings.

A luscious mango sauce is an exotic complement to this dark, velvety pâté. You can look for a canned version in Indian supermarkets. If desired, make your own by puréeing fresh mango with a little sugar and lime juice. Alternatively, serve the pâté on a thin pool of melted vanilla ice cream with an attractive garnish of fresh berries or just-thawed raspberries.

Per serving: about
- 260 calories
- 22 g fat
- 3 g protein
- 19 g carbohydrate

Chocolate Ice Cream

5	egg yolks	5
2/3 cup	granulated sugar	150 mL
1/2 cup	unsweetened cocoa powder	125 mL
1 cup	milk	250 mL
1 oz	unsweetened chocolate, chopped	30 g
2 cups	whipping cream	500 mL

● In large bowl, whisk egg yolks with sugar; set aside. In saucepan, whisk cocoa with 1/3 cup (75 mL) hot water until combined. Gradually whisk in milk; stir in chocolate. Cook over medium-high heat just until bubbles form around edge; gradually whisk into yolk mixture.

● Return egg mixture to pan; cook over medium-low heat, stirring constantly, for about 10 minutes or until thick enough to coat back of wooden spoon.

● Immediately strain through sieve into large bowl; stir in cream. Let cool to room temperature. Place waxed paper directly on surface; refrigerate for at least 2 hours or until chilled. *(Ice cream can be prepared to this point and refrigerated for up to 24 hours.)*

● Pour into shallow metal pan; cover and freeze for 3 to 4 hours or until almost firm. Break up into chunks; transfer to food processor and purée until smooth. Transfer to chilled airtight container; freeze for 1 hour or until firm. (Alternatively, freeze in ice-cream machine according to manufacturer's instructions.) *(Ice cream can be stored in freezer for up to 5 days.)* Transfer to refrigerator 30 minutes before serving. Makes about 4 cups (1 L).

I t's the combination of unsweetened chocolate and cocoa that heightens the chocolate sensation.

Per 1/2 cup (125 mL): about
- 350 calories
- 28 g fat
- 5 g protein
- 24 g carbohydrate

Mango and White Chocolate Mousse Terrine ▲

To make mango purée, cut
two opposite sides of
4 mangoes as close to pit as
possible. Cut grid pattern of
1/2-inch (1 cm) cubes in flesh
of each side down to (but not
through) skin; turn inside out.
Cut off cubes and place in
food processor. Cut remaining
mango away from pit; cube
and add to food processor.
Add 1/4 cup (50 mL)
granulated sugar and 1 tbsp
(15 mL) lime juice; purée
until smooth.

	MANGO MOUSSE	
2 cups	canned sweetened mango purée	500 mL
1 cup	whipping cream	250 mL
	WHITE CHOCOLATE MOUSSE	
8 oz	white chocolate, chopped	250 g
1 tsp	vanilla	5 mL
3/4 cup	whipping cream	175 mL

● MANGO MOUSSE: Place mango purée in
bowl. In separate bowl, whip cream; fold
half into purée. Fold in remaining whipped
cream. Set aside.

● WHITE CHOCOLATE MOUSSE: In bowl over
saucepan of hot (not boiling) water, melt
chocolate with vanilla, stirring occasionally;
let cool to room temperature. In separate
bowl, whip cream; fold half into chocolate.
Fold in remaining whipped cream.

● Line 8- x 4-inch (1.5 L) loaf pan with
plastic wrap, leaving enough overhang to
cover top. Spread half of the mango mousse
in pan; freeze for 15 minutes or until top is
firm. Spread white chocolate mousse on top;
freeze for 15 minutes or until top is firm.
Spread remaining mango mousse evenly
over top; cover with plastic wrap and freeze
for at least 6 hours or until firm throughout.
(Terrine can be overwrapped in foil and
frozen for up to 5 days.) Slice to serve.
Makes 8 servings.

Per serving: about • 375 calories • 3 g protein
• 29 g fat • 29 g carbohydrate

Frozen Hot Chocolate

1/3 cup	unsweetened cocoa powder	75 mL
2 oz	bittersweet chocolate, chopped	60 g
2/3 cup	whipping cream	150 mL
1/2 cup	granulated sugar	125 mL
1 tbsp	butter	15 mL
2 cups	milk	500 mL

● In saucepan, whisk together cocoa, chocolate, 1/4 cup (50 mL) of the cream, the sugar and butter; heat over low heat, whisking often, until chocolate and butter are melted and sugar is dissolved.

● Gradually whisk in milk and another 1/4 cup (50 mL) of the cream; bring just to boil. Pour into 9-inch (2.5 L) square cake pan. Let stand for 15 minutes. Wrap in plastic wrap or foil and freeze for at least 12 hours. *(Frozen chocolate can be prepared to this point and frozen in airtight container for up to 5 days.)*

● Let chocolate stand at room temperature for 5 minutes. Break into small pieces. Transfer to food processor along with remaining whipping cream; purée, scraping down side of bowl twice, until thick, smooth and creamy. Serve immediately in chilled goblets or refreeze for up to 30 minutes. Makes 4 servings.

*I*ced coffee? Frappuccino? *Why not frozen hot chocolate? Serve this cross between slush and ice cream in tall glasses with long spoons or thick straws.*

Per serving: about
- 400 calories
- 27 g fat
- good source of calcium
- 7 g protein
- 42 g carbohydrate

White Chocolate Apricot Ripple Ice Cream

1 cup	dried apricots	250 mL
6	egg yolks	6
1/3 cup	granulated sugar	75 mL
2 cups	18% cream	500 mL
6 oz	white chocolate, chopped	175 g
1 cup	whipping cream	250 mL
1 tsp	vanilla	5 mL

● In saucepan, bring apricots and 1 cup (250 mL) water to boil; reduce heat, cover and simmer, stirring occasionally, for 25 minutes or until apricots are very soft. Drain, reserving 1/2 cup (125 mL) liquid. In food processor, purée apricots with reserved liquid; cover and refrigerate for 1 hour or until chilled. *(Purée can be refrigerated in airtight container for up to 1 day.)*

● In large bowl, whisk egg yolks with sugar; set aside. In saucepan, heat 18% cream over medium-high heat just until bubbles form around edge; gradually whisk into yolk mixture. Return egg mixture to pan; cook over medium-low heat, stirring constantly, for about 10 minutes or until thick enough to coat back of wooden spoon.

● Immediately strain through sieve into large bowl. Add white chocolate; stir until melted. Stir in whipping cream and vanilla. Let cool to room temperature. Place waxed paper directly on surface; refrigerate for at least 2 hours or until chilled. *(Ice cream can be prepared to this point and refrigerated for up to 24 hours.)*

● Pour into shallow metal pan; cover and freeze for 3 to 4 hours or until almost firm. Break up into chunks; transfer to food processor and purée until smooth. (Alternatively, freeze in ice-cream machine according to manufacturer's instructions until frozen yet still soft enough to swirl.)

● Transfer one-quarter of the ice-cream mixture into chilled 6-cup (1.5 L) plastic freezer container. Using rubber spatula, swirl in one-quarter of the apricot purée. Repeat 3 times. Cover and freeze for 1 hour or until firm. *(Ice cream can be stored in freezer for up to 5 days.)* Transfer to refrigerator 30 minutes before serving. Makes about 5 cups (1.25 L).

*T*his frozen concoction is *delicious all on its own, but why not gild the lily with an indulgent drizzle of Chocolate Fudge Sauce (p. 58).*

Per 1/2 cup (125 mL): about
- 355 calories
- 26 g fat
- 5 g protein
- 27 g carbohydrate

Cookies Galore

Chocolate has managed to seduce cookie lovers with its sheer deliciousness, and the inventive recipes here chart new ways to go beyond the classics. Anyone for biscotti? Or chocolate salami?

Chocolate Chunk Shortbread ▶

At Desserts by Phipps, an always-crowded bakery and coffee shop in north Toronto, these chunky shortbread cookies are hands-down bestsellers.

Per cookie: about
- 100 calories
- 1 g protein
- 6 g fat
- 10 g carbohydrate

2-1/2 cups	all-purpose flour	625 mL
2 cups	butter, softened	500 mL
1 cup	instant dissolving (fruit/berry) sugar	250 mL
1 cup	sifted rice flour	250 mL
8 oz	milk chocolate, cut in chunks	250 g

● Spread 1-1/2 cups (375 mL) of the all-purpose flour on baking sheet; place under broiler 4 to 5 inches (10 to 12 cm) from heat. With oven door open, roast flour, turning with metal or wooden spatula every minute, for about 7 minutes or until medium brown color. Let cool to room temperature.

● In bowl, beat butter with sugar until light and fluffy. Sift together rice flour, roasted flour and remaining all-purpose flour; stir vigorously into butter mixture until well blended. Refrigerate for 1 hour. Stir in chocolate.

● Roll dough into 1-1/4-inch (3 cm) balls. Place on ungreased baking sheets, about 2 inches (5 cm) apart; flatten slightly. Bake in center of 275°F (140°C) oven for 50 minutes or until light golden. Let cool on sheets on rack. *(Cookies can be stored in airtight container for up to 5 days.)* Makes about 72 cookies.

Double Chocolate Shortbread

Two hits of chocolate guarantee satisfaction in these handy refrigerator cookies.

Per cookie: about
- 55 calories
- 1 g protein
- 4 g fat
- 5 g carbohydrate

1 cup	unsalted butter, softened	250 mL
1/3 cup	granulated sugar	75 mL
1 tsp	vanilla	5 mL
2 oz	semisweet chocolate, melted and cooled	60 g
1-2/3 cups	all-purpose flour	400 mL
1/3 cup	unsweetened cocoa powder	75 mL

● In large bowl, beat butter until fluffy; gradually beat in sugar and vanilla. Stir in chocolate. With wooden spoon, stir in flour and cocoa, about 1/4 cup (50 mL) at a time.

● Scoop onto two sheets of waxed paper. Using paper as guide, roll into 8-inch (20 cm) long logs. Wrap in waxed paper and refrigerate for at least 1 hour or until firm. *(Dough can be overwrapped in plastic wrap and refrigerated for up to 5 days or frozen for up to 3 weeks. Let frozen dough stand at room temperature for 15 minutes.)*

● Cut logs into 1/4-inch (5 mm) thick slices; place on ungreased baking sheets. Bake in center of 275°F (140°C) oven for 40 to 50 minutes or until firm to the touch. Let cool on sheets on rack for 10 minutes. Transfer to racks and let cool completely. Makes about 60 cookies.

Cranberry White Chocolate Oatmeal Cookies

These are not your everyday oatmeal cookies by any means — and a jar of them, tied with a bow, is the kind of present you just can't buy.

Per cookie: about
- 120 calories
- 1 g protein
- 5 g fat
- 16 g carbohydrate

1/2 cup	shortening, softened	125 mL
1/2 cup	butter, softened	125 mL
1 cup	packed brown sugar	250 mL
1/2 cup	granulated sugar	125 mL
1	egg	1
1 tsp	vanilla	5 mL
2 cups	quick-cooking rolled oats	500 mL
1-1/2 cups	all-purpose flour	375 mL
1/2 tsp	baking soda	2 mL
1/2 tsp	salt	2 mL
Pinch	cinnamon	Pinch
1 cup	dried cranberries	250 mL
5 oz	white chocolate, chopped	150 g

● In large bowl, beat together shortening, butter and brown and granulated sugars until light and fluffy. Beat in egg and vanilla. Stir together rolled oats, flour, baking soda, salt and cinnamon; stir into butter mixture, one-third at a time. Stir in cranberries and white chocolate.

● Drop by heaping tablespoonfuls (15 mL), about 2 inches (5 cm) apart, onto greased baking sheets; flatten slightly with floured fork. Bake in center of 350°F (180°C) oven for 12 to 14 minutes or until golden brown. Transfer to racks and let cool. *(Cookies can be stored in airtight container for up to 1 week or frozen for up to 2 weeks.)* Makes 48 cookies.

Crunchy Oatmeal Chippers ▼

By using miniature chocolate chips or chopping regular chips, you spread the chips throughout the batter, guaranteeing a satisfying chunk of chocolate in every bite. Corn syrup replaces some of the fat in these deliciously crisp cookies.

Per cookie: about
- 80 calories
- 1 g protein
- 2 g fat
- 13 g carbohydrate

1/4 cup	butter, softened	50 mL
3/4 cup	packed brown sugar	175 mL
1	egg	1
1/3 cup	corn syrup	75 mL
2 tsp	vanilla	10 mL
1-3/4 cups	large-flake rolled oats	425 mL
1 cup	all-purpose flour	250 mL
1 tsp	baking powder	5 mL
1/4 tsp	salt	1 mL
1/3 cup	miniature chocolate chips	75 mL

● In large bowl, beat butter with sugar just until sugar is moistened; beat in egg, corn syrup and vanilla. In separate bowl, stir together oats, flour, baking powder and salt; stir in chocolate chips. Stir into butter mixture.

● Drop by tablespoonfuls (15 mL), about 2 inches (5 cm) apart, onto parchment paper- or foil-lined baking sheets; flatten slightly. *(Cookies can be prepared to this point, frozen on sheets until firm, then transferred to airtight containers and frozen for up to 1 week. Do not thaw; increase baking time to 12 minutes.)*

● Bake in center of 375°F (190°C) oven for 10 minutes or until lightly browned but still soft. Let cool on sheets on rack for 3 minutes; transfer to racks and let cool completely. *(Cookies can be stored in airtight container for up to 5 days or frozen for up to 1 month.)* Makes 36 cookies.

Double-Chocolate Drop Cookies

1 tbsp	instant coffee granules	15 mL
1 tbsp	vanilla	15 mL
2 cups	all-purpose flour	500 mL
1/2 cup	unsweetened cocoa powder	125 mL
1 tbsp	baking powder	15 mL
1/4 tsp	salt	1 mL
1	egg	1
2	egg whites	2
3/4 cup	granulated sugar	175 mL
3/4 cup	packed brown sugar	175 mL
1/4 cup	butter, melted	50 mL
3 tbsp	corn syrup	50 mL
1 cup	chocolate chips	250 mL

● Dissolve coffee granules in vanilla; set aside. Stir together flour, cocoa, baking powder and salt; set aside.

● In large bowl, beat together egg, egg whites and granulated and brown sugars until light and foamy. Beat in butter, corn syrup and coffee mixture. Gradually beat in flour mixture, 1/2 cup (125 mL) at a time, until well combined. Stir in chocolate chips.

● Drop by tablespoonfuls (15 mL), about 2 inches (5 cm) apart, onto nonstick or parchment paper-lined baking sheets. Bake in center of 350°F (180°C) oven for 8 to 10 minutes or until firm. Let cool on sheets on rack for 2 minutes. Transfer to racks and let cool completely. *(Cookies can be stored in airtight container for up to 5 days or frozen for up to 2 weeks.)* Makes 60 cookies.

VARIATIONS

● DOUBLE-CHOCOLATE MINT COOKIES: Substitute 3/4 tsp (4 mL) mint extract for coffee granules; combine with vanilla.

● DOUBLE-CHOCOLATE ORANGE COOKIES: Substitute 2 tsp (10 mL) grated orange rind for coffee granules; combine with vanilla.

Rich in chocolate flavor from cocoa powder, these dense cake-like cookies have less than half the fat of a regular crisp chocolate chip cookie.

Per cookie: about
- 65 calories
- 2 g fat
- 1 g protein
- 11 g carbohydrate

Chocolate Kisses

3	egg whites	3
Pinch	salt	Pinch
3/4 cup	granulated sugar	175 mL
3/4 cup	miniature semisweet chocolate chips	175 mL
1/2 tsp	potato starch or cornstarch	2 mL
1/2 tsp	vanilla	2 mL

● In bowl, beat egg whites with salt until soft peaks form. Beat in sugar, 2 tbsp (25 mL) at a time, until stiff shiny peaks form. Sprinkle with chocolate chips, potato starch and vanilla; gently fold into egg whites.

● Using pastry bag fitted with 1-inch (2.5 cm) opening, or 2 spoons, pipe 1-inch (2.5 cm) kisses onto two parchment paper- or foil-lined baking sheets. Bake in top and bottom thirds of 300°F (150°C) oven, switching and rotating pans halfway through, for 25 to 30 minutes or just until firm to the touch. Transfer to racks and let cool. *(Cookies can be stored in airtight container for up to 4 days.)* Makes about 40 cookies.

Light as a spring breeze, these sweet meringue cookies are a delicious tradition for Passover.

Per cookie: about
- 30 calories
- 1 g fat
- trace protein
- 6 g carbohydrate

Chocolate Nut Biscotti

If you've been tempted by the trendy but pricey biscotti in a coffee shop, try your hand at these long, crunchy ones from the kitchen of Carol Ferguson.

Per cookie: about
- 115 calories
- 2 g protein
- 6 g fat
- 13 g carbohydrate

2/3 cup	granulated sugar	150 mL
1/3 cup	butter, softened	75 mL
2 tbsp	vegetable oil	25 mL
2	eggs	2
1-1/2 tsp	vanilla	7 mL
1/2 tsp	almond extract	2 mL
1-1/2 cups	all-purpose flour	375 mL
1/2 cup	sifted unsweetened cocoa powder	125 mL
2 tsp	baking powder	10 mL
1/2 tsp	salt	2 mL
1/2 cup	coarsely chopped almonds or hazelnuts	125 mL

● In bowl, beat together sugar, butter and oil until light and fluffy. Beat in eggs, one at a time; beat in vanilla and almond extract. Stir together flour, cocoa, baking powder and salt; stir into butter mixture to make soft, sticky dough. Stir in nuts.

● Turn dough out onto lightly floured surface; with floured hands, knead into smooth ball. Divide in half; shape each half into log about 6 inches (15 cm) long. Place logs about 4 inches (10 cm) apart on greased baking sheets. Flatten each log to about 3 inches (8 cm) wide, leaving top slightly rounded.

● Bake in center of 325°F (160°C) oven for about 30 minutes or until pale golden and not quite firm to the touch. Let cool on baking sheets on rack for 3 minutes.

● Using long spatula, transfer to cutting board; using large, sharp knife, slice diagonally into 1/2-inch (1 cm) thick slices. Spread out slices upright, about 1 inch (2.5 cm) apart, on baking sheets. Bake for about 35 minutes or until golden, firm and dry. Let cool on sheets on rack. *(Biscotti can be stored in airtight container for up to 1 week.)* Makes about 24 cookies.

Soft and Chewy Chocolate Orange Cookies

Get the kids to help make these easy-to-roll cookies. They'll have fun choosing and pressing out their favorite shapes — stars and santas for Christmas, dreidels and menorahs for Hanukkah, or all the animals in the zoo for a birthday party.

Per cookie: about
- 55 calories
- 1 g protein
- 2 g fat
- 8 g carbohydrate

1/2 cup	butter	125 mL
1 cup	icing sugar	250 mL
1-1/2 tsp	grated orange rind	7 mL
1	egg	1
2 tbsp	orange juice concentrate	25 mL
1-3/4 cups	all-purpose flour	425 mL
1/2 cup	unsweetened cocoa powder	125 mL
2 tsp	baking powder	10 mL
1/4 cup	granulated sugar	50 mL

● In bowl, beat together butter, icing sugar and orange rind until light and fluffy. Beat in egg and orange juice concentrate.

● Stir together flour, cocoa and baking powder; stir into butter mixture just until combined. Divide dough in half; flatten into discs. Wrap each in plastic wrap; refrigerate for about 2 hours or until well chilled.

● On lightly floured surface, roll out each disc to 1/8-inch (3 mm) thickness. With 3-inch (8 cm) cookie cutter, cut out shapes; sprinkle with granulated sugar. Place cutouts, about 1/2 inch (1 cm) apart, on greased baking sheets. *(Cookies can be prepared to this point, covered and refrigerated for up to 24 hours.)*

● Bake in center of 350°F (180°C) oven for about 10 minutes or until cookies are almost firm to the touch. Transfer to racks and let cool. *(Cookies can be stored in airtight container for up to 3 days.)* Makes about 48 cookies.

Brutti ma Buoni

2-1/4 cups	hazelnuts	550 mL
4	egg whites	4
1-1/4 cups	granulated sugar	300 mL
1/2 tsp	vanilla	2 mL
2 oz	semisweet chocolate, chopped	60 g

● Toast hazelnuts on baking sheet in center of 350°F (180°C) oven for 5 to 10 minutes or until fragrant. Transfer to tea towel; rub off as much of the skins as possible. Transfer to food processor; using on/off motion, chop coarsely. Set aside.

● In large heatproof bowl over gently simmering water, whisk together egg whites and sugar; cook, whisking occasionally, for about 10 minutes or until hot and opaque. Remove from heat; beat for about 7 minutes or until thick and glossy. Stir in vanilla. Stir in hazelnuts.

● Drop by heaping tablespoonfuls (15 mL), about 2 inches (5 cm) apart, onto parchment paper-lined baking sheets. Bake in center of 350°F (180°C) oven for 25 to 30 minutes or until light brown and dry in center. Transfer to racks and let cool.

● In bowl over saucepan of hot (not boiling) water, melt chocolate, stirring occasionally; using fork, drizzle over cookies. *(Cookies can be stored in airtight container for up to 5 days.)* Makes about 30 cookies.

*"U*gly but good" may be the literal translation, but these chewy hazelnut and chocolate cookies are definitely more than just "good."*

Per cookie: about
- 120 calories
- 2 g protein
- 8 g fat
- 11 g carbohydrate

Chocolate Salami ▼

16	shortcake or butter cookies (7 oz/200 g)	16
8 oz	semisweet chocolate, chopped	250 g
1/4 cup	butter	50 mL
3 tbsp	whipping cream or 18% cream	50 mL
1/3 cup	each raisins and chopped dried apricots	75 mL
1/4 cup	pine nuts	50 mL

● In food processor, or in plastic bag and using rolling pin, crush cookies until broken into crumbs with some small chunks to make 1-1/2 cups (375 mL); set aside.

● In bowl over saucepan of hot (not boiling) water, melt together chocolate, butter and cream, stirring occasionally. Stir in cookie crumbs and chunks, raisins, apricots and pine nuts. Let cool completely.

● Place chocolate mixture on plastic wrap; using wrap, roll into 10-inch (25 cm) long log. Wrap again in plastic wrap. Refrigerate until chilled. *(Chocolate salami can be refrigerated for up to 5 days or frozen in airtight container for up to 2 weeks; let stand at room temperature for 10 minutes.)* Slice thinly to serve. Makes about 24 slices.

Per slice: about • 135 calories • 2 g protein • 9 g fat
• 14 g carbohydrate

*T*his salami-shaped chocolate confection slices neatly and looks irresistible on any pastry tray.*

Crunchy Chocolate Peanut Butter Chunks

The secret to this very crunchy cookie is to gradually stir the flour into the butter mixture, then bring the dough together by handfuls before patting it into the pan. Do not grease the pan, or the underside of the cookie will fry.

Per piece: about
- 95 calories
- 5 g fat
- 2 g protein
- 11 g carbohydrate

1 cup	butter, softened	250 mL
1/3 cup	smooth peanut butter	75 mL
1-1/2 cups	granulated sugar	375 mL
2 tsp	vanilla	10 mL
3 cups	all-purpose flour	750 mL
Pinch	salt	Pinch
1 cup	each semisweet chocolate chips and peanut butter chips	250 mL
3 oz	bittersweet chocolate, chopped	90 g

● In large bowl, beat butter with peanut butter; gradually beat in sugar until light and fluffy. Beat in vanilla. In separate bowl, mix flour with salt; using wooden spoon, very gradually stir into butter mixture until combined. Stir in chocolate chips and peanut butter chips.

● Gently squeeze dough in handfuls until dough holds together; pat into ungreased 17- x 11-inch (45 x 29 cm) rimmed baking sheet. Bake in center of 350°F (180°C) oven for 30 to 40 minutes or until firm to the touch and golden. Let cool on sheet on rack.

● In bowl over saucepan of hot (not boiling) water, melt chocolate, stirring occasionally. Drizzle over cookie. Let cool completely. Break into pieces. Makes 72 pieces.

Peanut Butter Chocolate Swirl Cookies ▼

First it was icebox cookies, then refrigerator cookies, now these logs of ready-to-bake dough are called freezer cookies. How easy technology makes it for us to keep the cookie jar full! Just slice and bake whenever the urge for cookies strikes.

Per cookie: about
- 65 calories
- 3 g fat
- 1 g protein
- 7 g carbohydrate

6 oz	bittersweet chocolate, chopped	175 g
2/3 cup	butter, softened	150 mL
2/3 cup	peanut butter	150 mL
1-1/3 cups	granulated sugar	325 mL
1	egg	1
1-1/2 tsp	vanilla	7 mL
2-1/3 cups	all-purpose flour	575 mL
3/4 tsp	baking soda	4 mL
1/4 tsp	salt	1 mL

● In bowl over saucepan of hot (not boiling) water, melt chocolate, stirring occasionally. Set aside.

● In large bowl, beat together butter, peanut butter and sugar until smooth; beat in egg and vanilla. Stir together flour, baking soda and salt; stir into butter mixture in two additions.

● Divide dough into thirds. Scrape one-third onto large piece of waxed paper; cover with another piece of waxed paper. Roll out into 10- x 8-inch (25 x 20 cm) rectangle. Remove top paper. Spread with one-third of the chocolate. Using paper as guide, tightly roll up jelly roll-style. Remove paper. Wrap in plastic wrap, twisting ends to seal.

● Repeat with remaining dough and chocolate. Refrigerate for at least 3 hours or until firm. *(Logs can be refrigerated for up to 3 days or frozen in airtight container for up to 2 weeks; let thaw for 20 minutes.)*

● Cut into 1/4-inch (5 mm) thick slices; place on greased baking sheets. Bake in center of 375°F (190°C) oven for 10 to 15 minutes or until light golden. Let cool on sheets on rack for 5 minutes. Transfer to racks and let cool completely. *(Cookies can be stored in airtight container for up to 5 days or frozen for up to 3 weeks.)* Makes about 84 cookies.

Fudgy Chocolate Chip Cookies

10 oz	semisweet chocolate, chopped	300 g
1 cup	granulated sugar	250 mL
1 cup	packed brown sugar	250 mL
3/4 cup	butter, softened and cubed	175 mL
2	eggs, lightly beaten	2
1 tsp	vanilla	5 mL
1-3/4 cups	all-purpose flour	425 mL
1 tsp	baking soda	5 mL
1 cup	semisweet chocolate chips	250 mL

● In food processor, chop together chocolate and granulated and brown sugars until chocolate is powdery. Add butter; pulse until well combined.

● Pour in eggs and vanilla; blend until completely moist, scraping down bowl once.

Add flour and baking soda; pulse until blended. Transfer to bowl; stir in chocolate chips. *(Dough can be wrapped in plastic wrap and refrigerated for up to 3 days. Or place in heaping tablespoonfuls/15 mL on baking sheet and freeze; transfer to rigid airtight container and store for up to 2 weeks. Bake frozen, adding 2 minutes to baking time.)*

● Place by heaping tablespoonfuls (15 mL), about 2 inches (5 cm) apart, on greased baking sheets. Bake, one sheet at a time, in center of 350°F (180°C) oven for about 12 minutes or until puffed and set around edge but still soft in center. Let cool on sheets on rack for 5 minutes. Transfer to racks and let cool completely. *(Cookies can be stored in airtight container for up to 3 days.)* Makes about 50 cookies.

Only *in the food processor? Yes, only in the food processor. But these cookies are so tender and packed with melted chocolate and chips, they're worth the price of an appliance.*

Per cookie: about
- 125 calories
- 6 g fat
- 1 g protein
- 17 g carbohydrate

HOW TO MEASURE FOR BEST RESULTS

Careful measuring of ingredients is important for best results when baking.
Also, be sure you consistently follow either the imperial or the metric system throughout
the recipe — never a combination of the two.

Tools of the Trade
● There are two types of measuring cups: dry-ingredient and liquid-ingredient. Dry-ingredient measures come in sets of graduated sizes in imperial (1/4 cup, 1/3 cup, 1/2 cup and 1 cup) and metric (50 mL, 75 mL, 125 mL, 250 mL). Levels are marked on the outside of liquid-ingredient measures, with enough space below the rim to prevent spills.

● Measuring spoons are used for both dry and liquid ingredients. Imperial measures are 1/4 tsp, 1/2 tsp, 1 tsp, 1 tbsp; metric measures are 1 mL, 2 mL, 5 mL, 15 mL.

For Good Measure
● **Dry Ingredients:** Lightly spoon dry ingredient into measure, filling until heaping. Level off by running straight edge of knife across top. Do not pack or tap measure when filling. (If flour is packed, you could end up with 1/4 cup/50 mL more than called for.) Brown sugar, however, should be packed down until it holds the shape of the measure when it is turned out.

● **Fat Ingredients:** For soft fats, press firmly into dry measure, then level off top. For butter and other firm fats, use handy package markings as guides to slice off the amount needed. When there are no markings, use the displacement method: if a recipe calls for 1/2 cup (125 mL) butter, fill measuring cup with 1/2 cup (125 mL) water; submerge enough butter to make water level rise to 1 cup (250 mL). Drain off water.

● **Liquid Ingredients:** Place liquid measure on counter; pour in liquid to desired level, bending down to check measurement at eye level and pouring out or adding as necessary.

Chocolate Crinkle Cookies

The surface of these cake-like cookies cracks, revealing a zigzag of dark chocolate against the white icing-sugar coating.

Per cookie: about
- 105 calories
- 2 g protein
- 5 g fat
- 16 g carbohydrate

1/3 cup	butter	75 mL
4 oz	semisweet chocolate, chopped	125 g
3 oz	unsweetened chocolate, chopped	90 g
1-1/4 cups	granulated sugar	300 mL
3	eggs	3
2 tsp	vanilla	10 mL
1-1/2 cups	all-purpose flour	375 mL
2 tbsp	unsweetened cocoa powder	25 mL
1/2 tsp	baking powder	2 mL
Pinch	salt	Pinch
3/4 cup	icing sugar	175 mL

● In heavy saucepan, melt together butter and semisweet and unsweetened chocolates, stirring occasionally. Remove from heat. Whisk in sugar. Whisk in eggs, one at a time, whisking well after each addition. Whisk in vanilla.

● Stir together flour, cocoa, baking powder and salt; gradually stir into chocolate mixture until blended. Place plastic wrap directly on surface; refrigerate for at least 30 minutes or until firm or for up to 8 hours.

● Sift icing sugar onto shallow plate. With hands, roll heaping tablespoonfuls (15 mL) of dough into balls. Roll in icing sugar to coat completely. With slotted spoon, arrange, about 2 inches (5 cm) apart, on greased baking sheets. With fingers, flatten cookies slightly.

● Bake, one sheet at a time, in center of 325°F (160°C) oven for about 15 minutes or until firm outside but still soft inside. Let cool on sheets on rack for 5 minutes. Transfer to racks and let cool completely. *(Cookies can be stored in airtight container for up to 3 days.)* Makes about 36 cookies.

Double Chocolate Cookies

Cocoa and chopped white chocolate in the dough deliver a double hit of chocolate. For a triple hit, add a drizzle of dark chocolate.

Per cookie: about
- 55 calories
- 1 g protein
- 3 g fat
- 6 g carbohydrate

1 cup	butter, softened	250 mL
1 cup	granulated sugar	250 mL
1	egg	1
2 tsp	vanilla	10 mL
2-1/4 cups	all-purpose flour	550 mL
1/2 cup	unsweetened cocoa powder	125 mL
1/2 tsp	baking powder	2 mL
1/4 tsp	salt	1 mL
5 oz	white chocolate, chopped	150 g

● In bowl, beat butter with sugar until light and fluffy; beat in egg and vanilla. In separate bowl, stir together flour, cocoa, baking powder and salt; using wooden spoon, stir into butter mixture in two additions. Stir in white chocolate.

● Divide dough into thirds; scrape one-third onto large piece of waxed paper. Using paper as guide, roll into 8-inch (20 cm) long log. Remove paper. Wrap in plastic wrap, twisting ends to seal.

● Repeat with remaining dough. Refrigerate for at least 3 hours or until firm. *(Logs can be refrigerated for up to 3 days or frozen in airtight container for up to 3 weeks; let thaw for 20 minutes.)*

● Cut into 1/4-inch (5 mm) thick slices; place on greased baking sheets. Bake in center of 375°F (190°C) oven for 10 to 15 minutes or until light brown. Let cool on sheets on racks for 5 minutes. Transfer to racks and let cool completely. *(Cookies can be stored in airtight container for up to 5 days or frozen for up to 3 weeks.)* Makes about 84 cookies.

Soft and Chewy Chocolate Chip Cookies

1 cup	butter, melted and cooled	250 mL
1 cup	packed brown sugar	250 mL
3/4 cup	granulated sugar	175 mL
2	eggs	2
2 tsp	vanilla	10 mL
3 cups	all-purpose flour	750 mL
3/4 tsp	baking soda	4 mL
1	pkg (300 g) semisweet chocolate chips	1

● In large bowl, whisk together butter and brown and granulated sugars; beat in eggs, one at a time, beating well after each addition. Beat in vanilla.

● Stir flour with baking soda; with wooden spoon, stir into butter mixture, 1 cup (250 mL) at a time. With hands, mix in chocolate chips.

● Drop by heaping tablespoonfuls (15 mL), about 2 inches (5 cm) apart, onto greased baking sheets; freeze for about 1 hour or until firm.

● Bake in center of 350°F (180°C) oven for about 12 minutes or until lightly golden around edges but still soft in center. Let cool on sheets on rack for 5 minutes. Transfer to racks and let cool completely. *(Cookies can be stored in airtight container for up to 3 days.)* Makes about 48 cookies.

For all the fans of soft and chewy cookies, this one's for you!

Per cookie: about
- 130 calories
- 6 g fat
- 1 g protein
- 17 g carbohydrate

Gluten-Free Chocolate Chip Cookies

1/2 cup	butter, softened	125 mL
1/2 cup	granulated sugar	125 mL
1/4 cup	packed brown sugar	50 mL
1	egg	1
1 tsp	vanilla	5 mL
1/2 cup	whole bean flour	125 mL
1/4 cup	each rice flour and corn flour	50 mL
1 tsp	baking soda	5 mL
1/2 tsp	salt	2 mL
1 cup	chocolate chips	250 mL

● In bowl, beat together butter and granulated and brown sugars until light and fluffy; beat in egg and vanilla. Stir together bean, rice and corn flours, baking soda and salt; stir into butter mixture until blended. Stir in chocolate chips.

● Drop by teaspoonfuls (5 mL), about 2 inches (5 cm) apart, onto greased baking sheets. Bake in center of 350°F (180°C) oven for about 10 minutes or until golden brown. Let cool on sheets on rack. Makes about 48 cookies.

Home economist Kay Spicer developed these chocolate chip cookies using bean, rice and corn flours so people who can't tolerate gluten will be able to enjoy a tasty cookie along with everyone else.

Per cookie: about
- 60 calories
- 3 g fat
- 1 g protein
- 8 g carbohydrate

BROWNIE ICE CREAM BARS

For a dinner party, sandwich brownie layers around ice cream and slice.

● After cooling Chocolate Fudge Brownies (recipe, next page), omit dusting with icing sugar; cut in half instead of in squares. Transfer 3 cups (750 mL) ice cream to refrigerator; let soften for 30 minutes.
● Line 8- x 4-inch (1.5 L) loaf pan with plastic wrap, leaving enough excess to cover loaf. Place half of the brownie in pan; spread smoothly with ice cream. Top with remaining brownie half, pressing down slightly. Fold plastic wrap over top. Freeze for at least 4 hours or until solid. *(Wrapped loaf can be transferred to airtight container and frozen for up to 1 week.)*
● To serve, let loaf stand at room temperature for 10 minutes; slice into bars. Makes 8 servings.

Per serving: about • 465 calories • 6 g protein • 30 g fat • 50 g carbohydrate

Chocolate Fudge Brownies

It's hard to resist brownies when they're this deliciously dense and packed with chips. Try the master recipe, then discover how cherries, coffee and toasted walnuts give brownies a whole new meaning.

Per brownie: about
- 135 calories
- 8 g fat
- 2 g protein
- 15 g carbohydrate

3 oz	bittersweet chocolate, chopped	90 g
2 oz	unsweetened chocolate, chopped	60 g
1/3 cup	butter	75 mL
3/4 cup	granulated sugar	175 mL
2	eggs	2
2 tsp	vanilla	10 mL
1/2 cup	all-purpose flour	125 mL
Pinch	salt	Pinch
1/2 cup	semisweet chocolate chips	125 mL
1 tsp	icing sugar	5 mL

● In heavy saucepan, melt together bittersweet and unsweetened chocolates and butter, stirring occasionally. Let cool slightly.

● Whisk in sugar. Whisk in eggs, one at a time, whisking well after each addition; whisk in vanilla. Using wooden spoon, gradually stir in flour and salt. Stir in chocolate chips.

● Scrape into waxed paper-lined 8-inch (2 L) square cake pan. Bake in center of 350°F (180°C) oven for 25 to 30 minutes or until cake tester inserted in center comes out with just a few moist crumbs clinging to it. Let cool in pan on rack.

● Using sieve, dust with icing sugar; cut into squares. *(Brownies can be wrapped in plastic wrap and stored at room temperature for up to 3 days or frozen in rigid airtight container for up to 2 weeks.)* Makes 20 brownies.

VARIATIONS
● CHOCOLATE CHERRY BROWNIES: Substitute dried cherries for chocolate chips.

● NUTTY CHOCOLATE BROWNIES: Substitute 3/4 cup (175 mL) toasted chopped walnuts or pecans for the chocolate chips.

● COFFEE CHOCOLATE BROWNIES: Dissolve 1 tbsp (15 mL) instant espresso powder or coffee granules in vanilla. Omit chocolate chips. Garnish each baked brownie with chocolate-covered espresso bean.

Lean but Luscious Chocolate Brownies

When baking low-fat, an ingredient such as puréed plums, pears or apples provides the moisture and texture usually given by fat. (See photo, p. 55.)

Per brownie: about
- 95 calories
- 4 g fat
- 1 g protein
- 15 g carbohydrate.

2/3 cup	granulated sugar	150 mL
1/4 cup	butter, melted	50 mL
1	egg	1
2 tbsp	milk	25 mL
1-1/2 tsp	vanilla	7 mL
1/2 cup	all-purpose flour	125 mL
1/2 cup	unsweetened cocoa powder	125 mL
1/2 tsp	baking powder	2 mL
1/4 tsp	salt	1 mL
1	jar (4-1/2 oz/128 mL) strained baby food plums or pears (or 1/2 cup/125 mL puréed plums)	1

● In bowl, beat sugar with butter until combined but not smooth; beat in egg, milk and vanilla. In separate bowl, sift together flour, cocoa, baking powder and salt; using wooden spoon, stir into butter mixture alternately with plums, making two additions of flour mixture and one of plums. Spread in greased 8-inch (2 L) square cake pan, smoothing top.

● Bake in center of 350°F (180°C) oven for about 20 minutes or until cake tester inserted in center comes out with just a few moist crumbs clinging to it. Let cool completely in pan on rack. Cut into squares. *(Brownies can be refrigerated in airtight container for up to 3 days or wrapped in plastic wrap or foil and frozen for up to 1 week.)* Makes 16 brownies.

Cream Cheese Raspberry Brownies ▼

6 oz	semisweet chocolate, chopped	175 g
3 oz	unsweetened chocolate, chopped	90 g
2	pkg (250 g each) cream cheese, softened	2
2 cups	granulated sugar	500 mL
4	eggs	4
1 tbsp	vanilla	15 mL
1 cup	butter, softened	250 mL
1 cup	all-purpose flour	250 mL
1/4 tsp	salt	1 mL
1/2 cup	raspberry jam	125 mL

● In bowl over saucepan of hot (not boiling) water, melt semisweet and unsweetened chocolates, stirring occasionally. Let cool to lukewarm.

● In large bowl, beat cream cheese with 1/3 cup (75 mL) of the sugar until smooth. Beat in one of the eggs and 1 tsp (5 mL) of the vanilla until well combined. Set aside.

● In separate large bowl, beat butter with remaining sugar until smooth; beat in remaining eggs, one at a time, beating well after each addition. Beat in remaining vanilla, then chocolate, mixing well. Mix in flour and salt just until combined.

● Reserve 1 cup (250 mL) of the chocolate batter. Spread remaining chocolate batter in greased 13- x 9-inch (3.5 L) cake pan. Spread with cream cheese mixture. Spoon reserved chocolate batter in dollops over top. Spoon jam in smaller dollops among chocolate dollops. With knife, zigzag through layers to create marble effect.

● Bake in center of 350°F (180°C) oven for 35 minutes or until cake tester inserted 2 inches (5 cm) from center comes out with just a few moist crumbs clinging to it. Let cool on rack. Cut into squares. *(Brownies can be refrigerated in airtight container for up to 4 days.)* Makes 40 brownies.

You may have tasted cream cheese brownies before, but just wait until you try these. From Dufflet Rosenberg, a celebrated Toronto pastry chef — need we say more?

Per brownie: about
- 190 calories
- 2 g protein
- 12 g fat
- 19 g carbohydrate

White Chocolate Pecan Rum Balls

Whether you call it cookie or candy, this delicious new version of a confection classic keeps for a week in the refrigerator.

Per ball: about
- 80 calories
- 6 g fat
- 1 g protein
- 6 g carbohydrate

8 oz	white chocolate, chopped	250 g
2 cups	ground pecans (about 7 oz/200 g)	500 mL
1/4 cup	white rum	50 mL
1/4 cup	granulated sugar	50 mL

● In large bowl over saucepan of hot (not boiling) water, melt chocolate, stirring occasionally. Stir in pecans and rum. Cover and refrigerate for 20 minutes or until firm.

● Using two spoons, shape into 1-inch (2.5 cm) balls. Place sugar in bag; add rum balls and shake gently to coat evenly. *(Rum balls can be refrigerated in airtight container for up to 1 week.)* Serve chilled. Makes about 36 balls.

White Chocolate Cherry Pecan Bars

Bars and squares are no problem to make — no rolling, no dropping, no shaping. Here's a perfect example of how delicious and fuss-free a pan of these cake-style treats can be.

Per bar: about
- 155 calories
- 8 g fat
- 2 g protein
- 20 g carbohydrate

1/2 cup	unsalted butter, softened	125 mL
1 cup	packed brown sugar	250 mL
2	eggs	2
2/3 cup	sour cream	150 mL
1-1/2 tsp	vanilla	7 mL
2-1/4 cups	all-purpose flour	550 mL
1 tsp	baking powder	5 mL
1/2 tsp	each baking soda and salt	2 mL
6 oz	white chocolate, chopped	175 g
1 cup	dried cherries or cranberries	250 mL
1 cup	chopped pecans	250 mL
	TOPPING	
2 oz	white chocolate, chopped	60 g

● In bowl, beat butter with sugar until combined; beat in eggs, one at a time, beating well after each addition. Beat in sour cream and vanilla.

● In separate bowl, stir together flour, baking powder, baking soda and salt; stir into butter mixture, about 1/2 cup (125 mL) at a time. Gently stir in white chocolate, cherries and pecans.

● Scrape into greased 13- x 9-inch (3.5 L) cake pan; bake in center of 350°F (180°C) oven for about 20 minutes or until golden and cake tester inserted in center still has moist crumbs clinging to it. Let cool completely on rack.

● TOPPING: In bowl over saucepan of hot (not boiling) water, melt white chocolate, stirring occasionally; drizzle over cooled cake. Cut into bars. *(Bars can be stored in airtight container for up to 3 days or wrapped in plastic wrap or foil and frozen for up to 1 month.)* Makes 36 bars.

FREEZING COOKIES, BARS AND SQUARES

For cookies, bars or squares that can be frozen, layer them between sheets of waxed paper or plastic wrap in a rigid airtight container, then freeze them for up to the time specified in the recipe.

Cappuccino Cheesecake Squares

30	chocolate wafers	30
1 tbsp	butter, melted	15 mL
1 tbsp	instant espresso powder or coffee granules	15 mL
2 tsp	vanilla	10 mL
1	pkg (250 g) light cream cheese, softened	1
1 cup	1% cottage cheese	250 mL
1/2 cup	granulated sugar	125 mL
2	egg whites	2
1/4 cup	light sour cream	50 mL
2 tbsp	all-purpose flour	25 mL
2 tsp	unsweetened cocoa powder	10 mL
Pinch	cinnamon	Pinch

● In food processor, chop wafers into fine crumbs. Add butter and 1 tbsp (15 mL) water; whirl until crumbs are moistened. Press into greased 9-inch (2.5 L) square cake pan. Bake in center of 375°F (190°C) oven for about 10 minutes or until firm to the touch. Let cool.

● Meanwhile, dissolve espresso powder in vanilla; set aside. In food processor, blend together cream cheese, cottage cheese and sugar until smooth. Blend in egg whites, one at a time; blend in espresso mixture, sour cream and flour. Reserving 1/2 cup (125 mL), pour remaining cream cheese mixture over crust; tap pan on counter to remove air bubbles.

● Whisk cocoa and cinnamon into reserved cream cheese mixture until blended. Drizzle over batter; swirl with tip of knife to create marble effect.

● Set pan in larger shallow pan; pour in enough hot water to come 1 inch (2.5 cm) up sides. Bake in center of 325°F (160°C) oven for about 50 minutes or just until center is set. Remove pan from water; let cool on rack. Cover and refrigerate for about 2 hours or until cold. Cut into squares. *(Squares can be refrigerated in airtight container for up to 3 days or wrapped in plastic wrap or foil and frozen for up to 1 month.)* Makes 24 squares.

Elizabeth Baird loves to surprise and impress TV personality Dini Petty, and she did both when Dini tried these cheesecake squares on The Dini Show. Dini couldn't believe anything so rich-tasting was so low in fat! Freeze individual squares for upcoming desserts and treats. (See photo, p. 55.)

Per square: about
- 90 calories
- 3 g protein
- 4 g fat
- 10 g carbohydrate

Chocolate Toffee Squares

1/2 cup	slivered almonds	125 mL
1-3/4 cups	graham cracker crumbs	425 mL
1/2 cup	butter, melted	125 mL
1	can (300 mL) sweetened condensed milk	1
2 cups	semisweet chocolate chips	500 mL
1/2 cup	toffee pieces	125 mL

● Toast almonds on baking sheet in center of 350°F (180°C) oven for 5 to 10 minutes or until fragrant; let cool.

● In bowl, stir graham cracker crumbs with butter until well moistened; pat evenly into greased 13- x 9-inch (3.5 L) cake pan. Bake in center of 375°F (190°C) oven for about 7 minutes or until golden. Let cool on rack for 5 minutes.

● In small saucepan, stir together milk and 1 cup (250 mL) of the chocolate chips over low heat, stirring occasionally, for about 10 minutes or until chocolate is melted. Pour over prepared crust, spreading evenly. In bowl, stir together remaining chocolate chips and toffee pieces; sprinkle evenly over chocolate mixture. Top with toasted almonds.

● Bake in center of 350°F (180°C) oven for 15 to 20 minutes or just until edges start to bubble. Let cool in pan on rack. Cut into squares. *(Squares can be refrigerated in airtight container for up to 2 weeks; let stand for about 10 minutes before serving.)* Makes 30 squares.

These chewy squares will keep in the refrigerator for up to two weeks. Look for packaged toffee pieces in the bakery section of the supermarket — or use 1-1/2 packages (each 56 g) English toffee bars, broken into pieces.

Per square: about
- 180 calories
- 3 g protein
- 11 g fat
- 20 g carbohydrate

Queen of Sheba Squares ▼

Dense, almost fudge-like, these rich squares are particularly good served with fresh berries.

Per square: about
- 125 calories
- 2 g protein
- 10 g fat
- 8 g carbohydrate

3/4 cup	hazelnuts	175 mL
4 oz	bittersweet or semisweet chocolate, chopped	125 g
1/2 cup	butter, softened	125 mL
1/3 cup	granulated sugar	75 mL
3	eggs	3
1/2 cup	amaretti cookie crumbs (about 20 cookies)	125 mL
1 oz	white chocolate, chopped	30 g

● Toast hazelnuts on baking sheet in center of 350°F (180°C) oven for 5 to 10 minutes or until fragrant. Transfer to tea towel; rub off as much of the skins as possible. Chop finely and set aside.

● In bowl over saucepan of hot (not boiling) water, melt bittersweet chocolate, stirring occasionally; let cool slightly.

● In food processor, beat together butter, sugar and eggs for 3 minutes or until smooth. Add melted chocolate, cookie crumbs and hazelnuts; using on/off motion, blend well. Pour into greased 8-inch (2 L) square cake pan. Bake in center of 350°F (180°C) oven for 22 to 25 minutes or until top is firm to the touch. Let cool. (Cake will pull away from sides of pan.)

● In bowl over saucepan of hot (not boiling) water, melt white chocolate, stirring occasionally. Drizzle over cake; cut into squares. *(Squares can be refrigerated in airtight container for up to 5 days.)* Makes 20 squares.

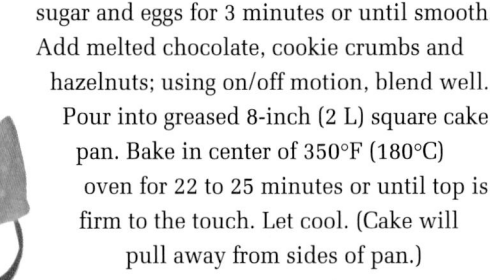

Cranberry Chocolate Bars

2 cups	large-flake rolled oats	500 mL
1 cup	packed brown sugar	250 mL
2/3 cup	all-purpose flour	150 mL
1/2 tsp	baking soda	2 mL
1/4 tsp	salt	1 mL
2/3 cup	butter, melted	150 mL
1 tsp	vanilla	5 mL
	TOPPING	
1 cup	butter	250 mL
4 oz	unsweetened chocolate, chopped	125 g
2 tsp	instant espresso powder or coffee granules	10 mL
4	eggs	4
1-1/2 cups	granulated sugar	375 mL
1/2 cup	all-purpose flour	125 mL
4 tsp	vanilla	20 mL
Pinch	salt	Pinch
1 cup	dried cranberries	250 mL

● In large bowl, stir together rolled oats, brown sugar, flour, baking soda and salt. Mix butter with vanilla; mix into dry ingredients until crumbly. Press into 13- x 9-inch (3.5 L) cake pan. Bake in center of 350°F (180°C) oven for 10 minutes.

● TOPPING: In heavy saucepan, heat together butter, chocolate and espresso powder over low heat until melted, stirring occasionally. Remove from heat. In large bowl, whisk together eggs, sugar, flour, vanilla and salt; stir in chocolate mixture and cranberries.

● Pour topping over hot crust; bake for 35 to 40 minutes or until edges are set and filling is still slightly soft. Let cool in pan on rack. Cut into bars. *(Bars can be refrigerated in airtight container for up to 5 days.)* Makes 40 bars.

Tangy-sweet dried cranberries are a refreshing complement to chocolate.

Per bar: about
● 185 calories ● 2 g protein
● 10 g fat ● 23 g carbohydrate

Chocolate Pecan Pie Squares

1-1/2 cups	all-purpose flour	375 mL
1/3 cup	icing sugar	75 mL
1/4 cup	unsweetened cocoa powder	50 mL
3/4 cup	cold unsalted butter, cubed	175 mL
1 tsp	vanilla	5 mL
1 tsp	cold water	5 mL
	TOPPING	
3 oz	unsweetened chocolate, chopped	90 g
1/3 cup	unsalted butter	75 mL
3/4 cup	packed brown sugar	175 mL
1	egg	1
3/4 cup	corn syrup	175 mL
1 tsp	vanilla	5 mL
3 cups	pecan halves	750 mL

● In food processor or bowl, combine flour, sugar and cocoa. Add butter, vanilla and water; pulse or cut in with pastry blender until fine crumbs form. With fingers, knead portions into balls of dough; press into greased 13- x 9-inch (3.5 L) cake pan. Bake in center of 350°F (180°C) oven for 20 minutes.

● TOPPING: Meanwhile, in bowl over saucepan of hot (not boiling) water, melt chocolate with butter, stirring occasionally; remove from heat. Whisk in sugar, then egg; whisk in corn syrup and vanilla. Stir in pecans. Pour over base, spreading evenly.

● Bake for 20 to 25 minutes or until filling is just set. Let cool completely in pan on rack. Refrigerate until firm. Cut along sides of pan; cut into squares. *(Squares can be refrigerated in airtight container for up to 5 days or wrapped in plastic wrap or foil and frozen for up to 1 month.)* Makes 48 squares.

For a double hit of chocolate, replace some of the flour in the pastry with unsweetened cocoa powder.

Per square: about
● 140 calories ● 1 g protein
● 10 g fat ● 13 g carbohydrate

Reverse Nanaimo Bars ▶

Reversing the order of the layers (the dark one is between the two light ones) gives a tasty new twist to a popular Canadian classic.

Per bar: about
- 165 calories
- 2 g protein
- 11 g fat
- 18 g carbohydrate

TIP: Be sure to use only pure white chocolate (either square or chips) rather than the less expensive kinds, which will not melt smoothly.

1 oz	white chocolate, chopped	30 g
1/4 cup	butter	50 mL
1	egg, beaten	1
1/2 cup	desiccated coconut	125 mL
1/4 cup	finely chopped almonds	50 mL
1-1/2 cups	graham cracker crumbs	375 mL
	MIDDLE LAYER	
1/3 cup	butter	75 mL
2/3 cup	sifted unsweetened cocoa powder	150 mL
1-1/3 cups	sifted icing sugar	325 mL
3 tbsp	milk	50 mL
2 tbsp	custard powder	25 mL
1 tsp	vanilla	5 mL
	TOP LAYER	
4 tsp	vegetable oil	20 mL
4 oz	white chocolate, chopped	125 g
1 oz	bittersweet chocolate, chopped	30 g

● In bowl over saucepan of hot (not boiling) water, melt white chocolate with butter, stirring occasionally. Stir in egg, coconut and almonds. Remove from heat; stir in crumbs. Press evenly into greased 8-inch (2 L) square cake pan; refrigerate.

● MIDDLE LAYER: In saucepan, melt butter over low heat; blend in cocoa. Transfer to bowl; beat in sugar, milk, custard powder and vanilla. Spread over bottom layer; refrigerate until firm.

● TOP LAYER: Reserve 1/4 tsp (1 mL) of the oil. In bowl over saucepan of hot (not boiling) water, melt white chocolate with remaining oil, stirring occasionally; pour over middle layer. Refrigerate until set.

● In bowl over saucepan of hot (not boiling) water, melt bittersweet chocolate with reserved oil, stirring occasionally. Drizzle over white chocolate. Refrigerate until set. Cut into bars. Makes 24 bars.

Panpepato Bars

Dare your guests to identify the secret ingredient in these sophisticated Italian-inspired squares — grape jelly!

Per bar: about
- 115 calories
- 2 g protein
- 5 g fat
- 16 g carbohydrate

1 cup	whole unblanched almonds	250 mL
1/2 cup	each pine nuts and walnuts	125 mL
3/4 cup	raisins	175 mL
3/4 cup	mixed chopped candied peel	175 mL
2/3 cup	all-purpose flour	150 mL
1 tsp	pepper	5 mL
3/4 tsp	cinnamon	4 mL
1/2 tsp	ground nutmeg	2 mL
1/4 tsp	ground cloves	1 mL
1/2 cup	liquid honey	125 mL
1/4 cup	grape jelly	50 mL
3 oz	bittersweet chocolate, chopped	90 g
3 tbsp	icing sugar	50 mL

● Toast almonds, pine nuts and walnuts on baking sheet in center of 350°F (180°C) oven for 10 minutes or until golden. Transfer to large bowl; add raisins and mixed peel. Set aside. In small bowl, stir together flour, pepper, cinnamon, nutmeg and cloves; set aside.

● In small saucepan, bring honey, grape jelly and 1 tbsp (15 mL) water to boil over medium-high heat, stirring. Remove from heat. Add chocolate; stir until melted. Stir into nut mixture until thoroughly coated. Stir in flour mixture just until combined.

● Scrape into greased 9-inch (2.5 L) square cake pan. Bake in center of 350°F (180°C) oven for about 30 minutes or until set, slightly darker and puffed. Let cool in pan on rack. Dust with icing sugar. Cut into bars. Makes 36 bars.

Sweets and Drinks

Ancient Aztecs believed chocolate was food for the gods. You'll know why, sipping a heavenly hot chocolate or nibbling a divine fudge, crunchy bark or smooth truffle.

White Chocolate and Cranberry Bark ▶

There are two new homemade chocolate candies — truffles and bark. And for both, the sky's the limit when it comes to flavors and add-ins. One of the more dramatic is cranberry and white chocolate, but you'll find takers for ginger and apricot, peanut and raisins and the tropical macadamia and dried pineapple, too. Most barks are as good with dark chocolate as with white. Use 1 lb (500 g) chocolate to about 2 cups (500 mL) of whatever additions you prefer.

Per piece: about
- 120 calories
- 7 g fat
- 2 g protein
- 13 g carbohydrate

1 lb	white chocolate, chopped	500 g
1 cup	each dried cranberries and shelled pistachios	250 mL

● In bowl over saucepan of hot (not boiling) water, melt chocolate, stirring occasionally. Stir in cranberries and pistachios.

● Pour onto foil-lined baking sheet; using palette knife or rubber spatula, spread into 12- x 8-inch (30 x 20 cm) rectangle. Refrigerate for at least 1 hour or until hardened. Break into pieces. *(Bark can be wrapped in plastic wrap and refrigerated in airtight container for up to 1 week.)* Makes 1-1/2 lb (750 g), about 32 pieces.

VARIATIONS

● FRUIT AND NUT CHOCOLATE BARK: Substitute semisweet or bittersweet chocolate for the white. Substitute 1 cup (250 mL) each unsalted roasted peanuts and raisins for the cranberries and pistachios.

● GINGER AND APRICOT WHITE CHOCOLATE BARK: Substitute 1-1/4 cups (300 mL) slivered dried apricots and 1/4 cup (50 mL) finely chopped candied ginger for the cranberries and pistachios.

● HAWAIIAN PLANTATION CHOCOLATE BARK: Substitute semisweet or bittersweet chocolate for the white. Substitute 2/3 cup (150 mL) chopped toasted macadamia or Brazil nuts and 1/2 cup (125 mL) each chopped dried pineapple and papaya for the cranberries and pistachios.

● MILK CHOCOLATE TOFFEE-PECAN BARK: Substitute milk chocolate for the white. Refrigerate 3 bars (56 g each) toffee until brittle; chop with large sharp knife and substitute along with 1 cup (250 mL) chopped toasted pecans for the cranberries and pistachios. (If desired, substitute 1 cup/250 mL chopped hard butterscotch candies or 1 pkg/225 g toffee bits for the 3 toffee bars.)

Clockwise from top: White Chocolate and Cranberry Bark; Macadamia Fudge (p. 82); candied Brazil nuts

Marble Chocolate Bark

8 oz	bittersweet chocolate, chopped	250 g
8 oz	white chocolate, chopped	250 g

● In two separate bowls over saucepans of hot (not boiling) water, melt bittersweet chocolate and white chocolate, stirring occasionally; let cool.

● Spoon onto foil-lined baking sheet in alternating patches to make 12- x 8-inch (30 x 20 cm) rectangle. With tip of knife, swirl chocolates into each other to create marble pattern. Refrigerate for at least 1 hour or until hardened. Break into pieces. *(Bark can be wrapped in plastic wrap and refrigerated in airtight container for up to 1 week.)* Makes 1 lb (500 g), about 32 pieces.

VARIATIONS

● MARBLE CHOCOLATE ALMOND BARK: Stir 3/4 cup (175 mL) toasted whole unblanched almonds into each saucepan of melted chocolate.

● BLACK FOREST CHOCOLATE BARK: Stir 3/4 cup (175 mL) dried cherries into each saucepan of melted chocolate.

Chocolate, Fruit and Nut Clusters

When presenting bark or clusters, choose pretty miniature paper cups and arrange them among dainty cookies on a sweet tray.

Per piece: about
• 100 calories   • 1 g protein
• 6 g fat   • 11 g carbohydrate

14 oz	semisweet or milk chocolate, chopped	400 g
1 cup	mixed nuts or peanuts	250 mL
1 cup	chopped dried or candied cherries, or cranberries or raisins	250 mL

● In bowl over saucepan of hot (not boiling) water, melt chocolate, stirring occasionally. Remove from heat. Stir in nuts and fruit.

● Drop by teaspoonfuls (5 mL), about 2 inches (5 cm) apart, onto two waxed paper-lined baking sheets. Refrigerate for 15 to 30 minutes or until chocolate is firm. *(Clusters can be layered between waxed paper and refrigerated in airtight container for up to 2 weeks.)* Makes 36 pieces.

Macadamia Fudge

How about a gift box of fudge? There's no sweeter way to make friends, encourage romance or deliver a genuine thank-you. *(See photo, p. 81.)*

Per piece: about
• 95 calories   • 1 g protein
• 7 g fat   • 9 g carbohydrate

8 oz	semisweet chocolate, chopped	250 g
3/4 cup	sweetened condensed milk	175 mL
1 tsp	vanilla	5 mL
1 cup	chopped macadamia nuts	250 mL

● In bowl over saucepan of hot (not boiling) water, melt chocolate with condensed milk, stirring occasionally. Stir in vanilla. Stir in nuts.

● Spread in foil-lined 8- x 4-inch (1.5 L) loaf pan. Refrigerate for at least 3 hours or until firm. Remove from pan and peel off foil; cut into small pieces. Makes 1-1/4 lb (625 g), about 32 pieces.

TIP: Other nuts, such as toasted pecans or California walnuts, can replace the macadamia.

Chocolate Pistachio Fudge

3 cups	icing sugar	750 mL
1/2 cup	unsweetened cocoa powder	125 mL
1/4 tsp	salt	1 mL
1/3 cup	18% cream	75 mL
1/2 cup	butter, cut in bits	125 mL
1/2 cup	semisweet chocolate chips	125 mL
2 tsp	vanilla	10 mL
1/4 cup	natural pistachios, finely chopped	50 mL

● In 12-cup (3 L) microwaveable bowl, stir together icing sugar, cocoa and salt; mix in cream. Scatter butter on top; microwave, uncovered, at High for 3 to 4 minutes or until steaming, stirring once. Stir in chocolate chips and vanilla until smooth. With electric mixer, beat for 3 to 4 minutes or until soft peaks form.

● Pour into foil-lined 8-inch (2 L) square cake pan. Sprinkle with pistachios; press in gently. Let cool to room temperature; refrigerate until firm.

● To cut into squares, heat knife under hot water and dry well before cutting. *(Fudge can be stored in airtight container for up to 3 days.)* Makes 25 squares.

Cook this make-ahead, super-quick fudge in the microwave, and leave time for the flavors to mellow.

Per square: about
- 120 calories
- 6 g fat
- 1 g protein
- 16 g carbohydrate

Chocolate Mice

4 oz	semisweet chocolate, chopped	125 g
1/3 cup	sour cream	75 mL
1 cup	fine chocolate wafer cookie crumbs	250 mL
1/3 cup	icing sugar or fine chocolate wafer cookie crumbs	75 mL
	GARNISH	
48	gold or silver dragées	48
48	almond slivers	48
24	pieces licorice shoestrings	24

● In bowl over saucepan of hot (not boiling) water, melt chocolate, stirring occasionally; let cool slightly. Stir in sour cream. Stir in cookie crumbs; mix well. Cover and refrigerate for about 1 hour or until firm.

● Roll scant tablespoonfuls (15 mL) into small balls slightly pointed at one end; roll lightly in icing sugar. Place on waxed paper-lined tray.

● GARNISH: Insert dragées for eyes, almond slivers for ears and small bits of licorice for tails. Refrigerate for about 2 hours or until firm. *(Chocolate mice can be refrigerated in airtight container for up to 1 week.)* Makes about 24 chocolates.

These mice, created by Margaret Fraser, have been one of our biggest hits ever. They're irresistible, eye-catching and lots of fun to make with kids young and old.

Per chocolate: about
- 65 calories
- 3 g fat
- 1 g protein
- 9 g carbohydrate

Chocolate Almond Brittle

For non-bakers, homemade candy is an ideal contribution to a bake sale. These crunchy, crackly pieces of chocolate-covered caramel brittle are sure to sell out immediately.

Per piece: about
- 215 calories
- 3 g protein
- 14 g fat
- 23 g carbohydrate

1 cup	sliced almonds	250 mL
1/2 cup	whole blanched almonds, chopped	125 mL
1/2 cup	unsalted butter	125 mL
1-1/3 cups	granulated sugar	325 mL
3 tbsp	water	50 mL
1 tbsp	white corn syrup	15 mL
6 oz	semisweet chocolate, finely chopped	175 g

● In heavy skillet, toast sliced almonds over medium heat, stirring occasionally, for about 4 minutes or until golden. Spread in foil-lined 13- x 9-inch (3.5 L) cake pan; set aside.

● Add chopped almonds to skillet; toast, stirring constantly, for 1 minute or until golden. Set aside.

● In saucepan, melt butter over medium heat; cook sugar, water and corn syrup, without stirring, until caramel-colored and candy thermometer registers 310°F (154°C).

● Immediately pour over sliced almonds, smoothing with back of greased metal spoon if necessary. Let cool for about 2 minutes or until set but still hot. Sprinkle with semisweet chocolate; spread with greased spoon. Sprinkle evenly with chopped almonds. Refrigerate until firm. Using tip of knife, break up into pieces. *(Brittle can be refrigerated in airtight container for up to 5 days.)* Makes 1-1/2 lb (750 g), about 18 pieces.

Hot Chocolate Mix

For hot chocolate any time, just add 1/4 cup (50 mL) mix to a mug of very hot milk and stir well.

Per 1/4 cup (50 mL): about
- 95 calories
- 4 g protein
- 1 g fat
- 20 g carbohydrate

2 cups	skim milk powder	500 mL
3/4 cup	granulated sugar	175 mL
1/2 cup	unsweetened cocoa powder	125 mL
1 tsp	cinnamon (optional)	5 mL
2 cups	mini marshmallows	500 mL

● Set sieve over large bowl; pour in skim milk powder, sugar, cocoa, and cinnamon (if using). Stir to combine and pass through sieve. Stir in marshmallows. *(Mix can be stored in airtight container at room temperature for up to 1 month.)* Makes about 4 cups (1 L).

Real Hot Chocolate

Melting chocolate in milk is not the conventional way to make hot chocolate in Canada — but it sure tastes great!

Per serving: about
- 315 calories
- 10 g protein
- 20 g fat
- 28 g carbohydrate
- excellent source of calcium

4 cups	milk	1 L
4 oz	semisweet chocolate, chopped	125 g
1/2 cup	whipped cream	125 mL

● In saucepan, heat milk over medium heat, stirring, until steaming; remove from heat. Add chocolate; whisk until smooth. Pour into warmed mugs; top with whipped cream. Makes 4 servings.

VARIATION

● WHITE HOT CHOCOLATE: Substitute 3 oz (90 g) chopped white chocolate for the semisweet. Add 1/4 cup (50 mL) liqueur or liquor (such as orange- or hazelnut-flavored liqueur or rum) after the chocolate is melted.

Chocolate Caramel Popcorn Nuggets

7 cups	popped corn	1.75 L
1/2 cup	packed brown sugar	125 mL
1/4 cup	butter	50 mL
2 tbsp	corn syrup	25 mL
1/4 tsp	each salt, baking soda and vanilla	1 mL
12 oz	bittersweet, milk or white chocolate, chopped	375 g

● Place popped corn in large greased metal bowl; set aside.

● In small saucepan, bring sugar, butter and corn syrup to boil over high heat; cook, stirring, for 2 minutes. Remove from heat; stir in salt, baking soda and vanilla. Pour over popped corn, tossing to coat.

● Working quickly, form heaping tablespoonfuls (15 mL) into balls; place 2 inches (5 cm) apart on two foil-lined baking sheets. Bake in center of 325°F (160°C) oven for 15 minutes. Let cool completely on sheets on racks.

● Meanwhile, in bowl over saucepan of hot (not boiling) water, melt chocolate, stirring occasionally. Spoon 1 tbsp (15 mL) over each mound. Refrigerate for about 30 minutes or until chocolate is firm. *(Nuggets can be refrigerated in airtight container for up to 2 days.)* Makes about 26 nuggets.

*W*hen the scary parts of the video are just too hair-raising, keep your eyes on a bowl of these "just-one-more" crunchy munchies.

Per nugget: about
- 110 calories
- 8 g fat
- 1 g protein
- 13 g carbohydrate

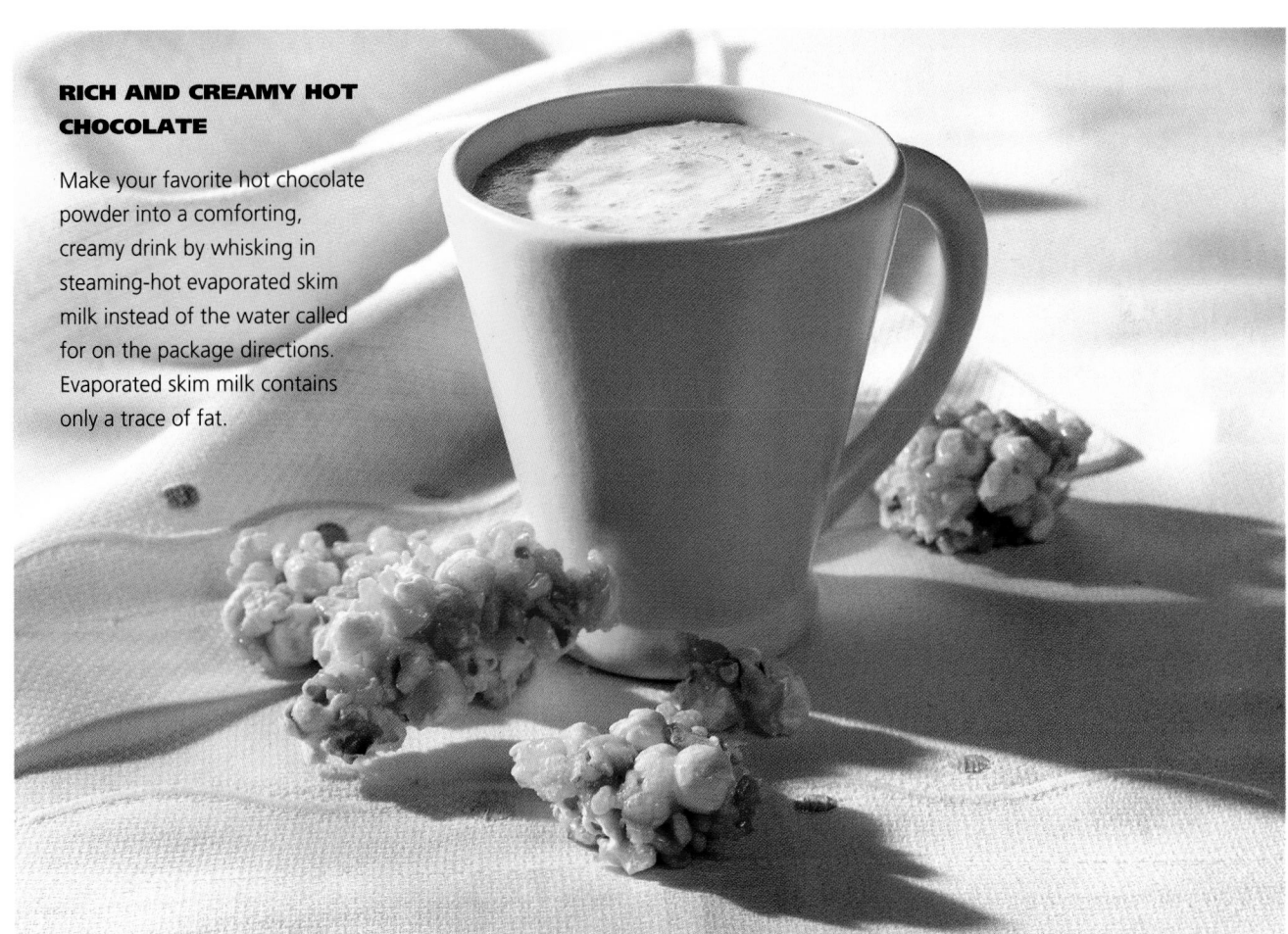

RICH AND CREAMY HOT CHOCOLATE

Make your favorite hot chocolate powder into a comforting, creamy drink by whisking in steaming-hot evaporated skim milk instead of the water called for on the package directions. Evaporated skim milk contains only a trace of fat.

Chocolate Truffles Galore ▼

Donna Bartolini created these superb truffles in the Canadian Living test kitchen — just about the most toothsome selection to make for serving with coffee or offering to favorite friends.

Per truffle: about
- 75 calories
- 6 g fat
- 1 g protein
- 7 g carbohydrate

8 oz	semisweet or bittersweet chocolate, chopped	250 g
2/3 cup	whipping cream	150 mL
2 tbsp	cold butter	25 mL
	COATING	
8 oz	semisweet or bittersweet chocolate, chopped	250 g
1/2 cup	unsweetened cocoa powder	125 mL

● Place chocolate in bowl. In small saucepan, heat cream with butter just until butter melts and bubbles form around edge of pan; pour into chocolate, whisking until smooth. Cover and refrigerate for 2 hours or until thickened and cold.

● Using melon baller or small spoon, scoop rounded teaspoonfuls (5 mL), dropping each onto waxed paper-lined tray. Press scraps together firmly; refrigerate for 30 minutes, then continue scooping until all scraps are used. (You may wish to press final bits into balls by hand.) Gently roll each ball between fingertips to round off completely. Freeze for about 1 hour or until hard and almost frozen.

● COATING: In bowl over saucepan of hot (not boiling) water, melt chocolate, stirring occasionally. Let cool slightly. Sift cocoa into pie plate. Using two forks, dip each ball into chocolate, letting excess drip off. (If chocolate thickens, rewarm gently.) Place balls in cocoa.

● Using two clean forks, roll truffles in cocoa; refrigerate on waxed paper-lined baking sheet until hardened. Place truffles in candy cups and refrigerate in airtight container until serving. *(Truffles can be refrigerated for up to 1 week or frozen for up to 3 months.)* Makes about 44 truffles.

VARIATIONS

● HAZELNUT TRUFFLES: Reduce cream to 1/2 cup (125 mL); add 3 tbsp (50 mL) hazelnut liqueur to melted chocolate filling. Coating: Omit cocoa powder. After rolling into rounded balls, roll in 1-1/2 cups (375 mL) finely chopped toasted hazelnuts; freeze and dip into chocolate as directed.

● ORANGE TRUFFLES: Reduce cream to 1/2 cup (125 mL); add 3 tbsp (50 mL) orange liqueur to melted chocolate filling.

● PEANUT BUTTER TRUFFLES: Omit butter. Add 1/4 cup (50 mL) smooth peanut butter to melted chocolate filling.

● RASPBERRY TRUFFLES: Reduce cream to 1/3 cup (75 mL). Press 1 cup (250 mL) fresh or thawed unsweetened raspberries through fine sieve to remove seeds and make 1/2 cup (125 mL) purée; add to melted chocolate filling.

Chocolate Caramel Truffles

1 cup	granulated sugar	250 mL
2/3 cup	whipping cream	150 mL
8 oz	bittersweet chocolate, chopped	250 g
1 tsp	vanilla	5 mL
2 tbsp	unsalted butter, softened	25 mL
1/4 cup	unsweetened cocoa powder	50 mL

● In heavy saucepan, cook sugar over medium heat, stirring, until melted; swirl pan until sugar is golden. Remove from heat. Carefully pour in cream in thin steady stream, stirring constantly and being careful to avoid spatters. Return to heat; simmer, stirring, until caramel is dissolved. Remove from heat.

● Stir in chocolate and vanilla; let stand for 5 minutes. Stir until chocolate is melted. Transfer to bowl; cover and refrigerate for at least 2 hours or until firm.

● Beat in butter until combined. Form into 1-inch (2.5 cm) balls and roll in cocoa, chilling mixture if it becomes too soft to hold its shape. Refrigerate on waxed paper-lined tray for about 1 hour or until firm. *(Truffles can be layered between waxed paper and refrigerated in airtight container for up to 2 weeks or frozen for up to 2 months.)* Makes 36 truffles.

T*o keep truffles firm, it's important to store them in the refrigerator. For a party, arrange the truffles in paper cups on a serving dish. Cover lightly and serve right from the refrigerator.*

Per truffle: about
- 75 calories
- 1 g protein
- 5 g fat
- 9 g carbohydrate

CHOCOLATE DIPPERS

Once you're in the mood to dip, there's plenty of choice. Fruit, including bananas and strawberries, is a classic. But how about pretzels? or coffee spoons?

CHOCOLATE COFFEE SPOONS

● In bowl over saucepan of hot (not boiling) water, melt 4 oz (125 g) chopped semisweet, milk or white chocolate, stirring occasionally. Remove from heat. Dip bowl of each of 8 heatproof plastic spoons into chocolate to completely coat. Refrigerate on waxed paper-lined baking sheet until firm. Wrap chocolate end of spoon in plastic wrap; tie with ribbon. *(Spoons can be refrigerated in airtight container for up to 2 weeks.)* Makes 8 spoons.

Per spoon: about • 75 calories • 1 g protein • 5 g fat • 8 g carbohydrate

CHOCOLATE-DIPPED PRETZELS

● In bowl over saucepan of hot (not boiling) water, melt 4 oz (125 g) chopped semisweet or white chocolate, stirring occasionally. Dip 2 cups (500 mL) mini pretzels, one at a time, halfway into chocolate. Refrigerate on waxed paper-lined baking sheet for 15 minutes or until chocolate is firm. Makes 50 pretzels.

Per pretzel: about
- 20 calories
- trace protein
- 1 g fat
- 3 g carbohydrate

CHOCOLATE FRUIT

● In bowl over saucepan of hot (not boiling) water, melt 3 oz (90 g) chopped semisweet or milk chocolate, stirring occasionally; let cool slightly. Cut one banana into 3/4-inch (2 cm) chunks. Dip 1 cup (250 mL) whole strawberries and banana chunks, one at a time, halfway into chocolate. Refrigerate on waxed paper-lined baking sheet until chocolate is firm. Makes 4 servings.

Per serving: about
- 150 calories
- 1 g protein
- 8 g fat
- 22 g carbohydrate

Chocolate Garnishes

The cutouts and chocolate curls featured here make enough to decorate an 8-inch (20 cm) cake.

● Using heavy knife, chop 8 oz (250 g) semisweet chocolate. In bowl over saucepan of hot (not boiling) water, melt chocolate, stirring occasionally.

SHEET METHOD
● Pour chocolate onto 15- x 10-inch (38 x 25 cm) rimmed baking sheet (do not use nonstick pan). With offset palette knife or rubber spatula, spread evenly over pan. Refrigerate until set, about 15 minutes. Place baking sheet on large damp towel that extends beyond edges of sheet; let stand for 3 minutes.

● **Short curls:** Brace pan against body. Holding bowl of teaspoon at 90-degree angle to pan and working toward yourself, scrape chocolate into curls, refrigerating pan if chocolate begins to soften. Use toothpick or spatula to transfer curls, in single layer, to waxed paper-lined baking sheet. Refrigerate.

● **Pencil-thin curls:** Brace pan against body. At opposite side of pan, hold large chef's knife at 90-degree angle to pan; hold top of blade firm and steady with other hand. Pull knife toward yourself, scraping chocolate into pencil-thin curls.

● **Long curls:** Let pan stand for 5 minutes; brace opposite side with hand. Holding stainless steel spatula or pastry scraper upside down at 45-degree angle, push spatula away from yourself, scraping chocolate into long curls.

● **Cutouts:** Spread chocolate over *half* of parchment- or waxed paper-lined baking sheet; refrigerate for 15 minutes. Let stand for 5 minutes. Using cookie cutter or sharp knife, cut out patterns. Lift off with knife: peel off paper, if necessary.

BLOCK METHOD

● Pour chocolate into foil-lined 5-3/4- x 3-1/4 inch (625 mL) loaf pan. Refrigerate for 2 hours or until set; unmould. Let stand for 20 minutes or until slightly soft.

● **Long, thin curls:** Holding chocolate block with piece of foil or waxed paper to prevent melting, coarsely grate one long side of chocolate into long, thin curls.

● **Short, thick curls:** Holding chocolate with foil, slowly draw blade of sharp vegetable peeler across either width or thin side of block.

Three-Layer Chocolate Fudge Cake (p. 6)

The Contributors

For your easy reference, we have included an alphabetical listing of recipes by contributor.

Julian Armstrong
Tarte au Chocolat, 38

Elizabeth Baird
Chocolate Tartlets, 46
Chocolate Walnut Butter
    Tart Pie, 44
Two-Chocolate Crème
    Brûlée, 58

Donna Bartolini
Chocolate Salami, 67
Panpepato Bars, 78

Johanna Burkhard
Nouvelle Bûche de Noël, 16

Pam Collacott
Chocolate Coffee Spoons, 87
Chocolate, Nut and Fruit
    Clusters, 82
Hot Chocolate Mix, 84

Cynthia David
Brutti ma Buoni, 67
Chocolate Chunk
    Shortbread, 62
Chocolate Pumpkin Pie, 41

Riki Dixon
Soft and Chewy Chocolate
    Orange Cookies, 66

Carol Ferguson
Chocolate Nut Biscotti, 66
Reverse Nanaimo Bars, 78

Margaret Fraser
Chocolate Mice, 83
Chocolate Pound Cake, 31

Ruth Gangbar
Chocolate Cake Finishes, 23

Heather Howe
Choco-Chip Buttermilk
    Loaf, 30
Chocolate Fondue with
    Banana Bread, 50
Cranberry White Chocolate
    Oatmeal Cookies, 64

Anne Lindsay
Chocolate Banana
    Cupcakes, 33
Chocolate Chip Coffee
    Cake, 27
Double-Chocolate Drop
    Cookies, 65
Easy Chocolate Snacking
    Cake, 30

Jennifer MacKenzie
Chocolate Peanut Butter
    Mousse Cake, 9

Jan Main
Cappuccino Torte, 14
Chocolate Prune Rum
    Cake, 28

Rose Murray
Chocolate Caramel
    Truffles, 87
Chocolate Ginger Tassies, 45
Chocolate Pecan
    Fruitcake, 24
Coffee Parfait Pie, 42
White Chocolate Pecan Rum
    Balls, 74

Daphna Rabinovitch
Chocolate Cookie
    Cheesecake, 18
Chocolate Indulgence
    Cake, 26
Chocolate Kisses, 65
Chocolate, Nut and Date
    Baklava, 46
Chocolate Pecan Pie
    Squares, 77
Chocolate Walnut Cake, 27
Frozen Hot Chocolate, 61
Fudge Truffle Tart, 38
Fudgy Chocolate Chip
    Cookies, 69
Light Chocolate Espresso
    Marble Cheesecake, 18
White Chocolate and
    Raspberry Parfait, 52
White Chocolate Cherry
    Pecan Bars, 74

Iris Raven
Chocolate Almond
    Brittle, 84
Chocolate Pistachio
    Fudge, 83

Dufflet Rosenberg
Cranberry Chocolate
    Bars, 77
Cream Cheese Raspberry
    Brownies, 73

Marianne Sanders
Chocolate Tiramisu
    Torte, 22

Kay Spicer
Gluten-Free Chocolate Chip
    Cookies, 71

Bonnie Stern
Chocolate Brownie Turtle
    Cake, 25

Joanne Yolles
Mocha Layer Cake, 15

Canadian Living Test Kitchen
Baked Chocolate Mousse, 56
Basic Butter Icing, 24
Best-Ever Chocolate Cream
    Pie, 42
Best-Ever Chocolate
    Icing, 24
Brownie Ice Cream Bars, 88
Cappuccino Cheesecake
    Squares, 75
Cheesecake Brownie
    Cupcakes, 33
Chocolate Almond Fruit
    Strudel, 45
Chocolate Banana
    Pudding, 54
Chocolate Bread
    Pudding, 51
Chocolate Caramel Popcorn
    Nuggets, 85
Chocolate Chestnut
    Mousse, 53
Chocolate Cloud Cake, 28

Chocolate Crinkle
Cookies, 70
Chocolate Espresso Angel
Cake, 31
Chocolate Fruit, 87
Chocolate Fudge
Brownies, 72
Chocolate Fudge Sauce, 58
Chocolate Garnishes, 88
Chocolate Hazelnut
Dacquoise, 8
Chocolate Ice Cream, 59
Chocolate Mousse-Filled
Hearts, 54
Chocolate Pâté, 59
Chocolate Pavlova, 20
Chocolate Pudding Cake, 51
Chocolate Raspberry
Dome, 10
Chocolate Soufflé, 48
Chocolate Steamed
Pudding, 53
Chocolate Toffee Squares, 75
Chocolate Truffles Galore, 86
Chocolate-Dipped
Pretzels, 87
Crunchy Chocolate Peanut
Butter Chunks, 68
Crunchy Oatmeal
Chippers, 64
Dark Chocolate
Cheesecake, 20

Double Chocolate
Shortbread, 62
Double Chocolate
Cookies, 70
Lean but Luscious Chocolate
Brownies, 72
Light Pots de Crème, 57
Macadamia Fudge, 82
Mango and White Chocolate
Mousse Terrine, 60
Marble Chocolate Bark, 82
Peanut Butter Chocolate
Swirl Cookies, 68
Queen of Sheba Squares, 76
Real Hot Chocolate, 84
Rich and Creamy Hot
Chocolate, 85
Soft and Chewy Chocolate
Chip Cookies, 71
Strawberry White Chocolate
Tart, 41
Three-Layer Chocolate Fudge
Cake, 6
Truffle Pots de Crème, 56
Very Berry Chiffon Pie, 37
White Chocolate and
Cranberry Bark, 80
White Chocolate Apricot
Ripple Ice Cream, 61
White Chocolate Carousel
Cake, 13
White Chocolate Lemon
Tart, 34

Photography Credits

FRED BIRD: pages 3
(bottom), 19, 25, 40, 44, 76,
83, 86, 88, 89.

DOUGLAS BRADSHAW:
pages 3 (middle), 21, 55,
64, 73.

PETER CHOU: page 36.

MICHAEL VISSER: page 81.

MICHAEL WARING: pages 3
(top), 4, 8, 29, 33, 35, 63, 79.

ROBERT WIGINGTON: front
cover; pages 7, 11, 12, 14,
17, 23, 32, 39, 43, 47, 49, 50,
53, 60, 67, 68, 85, 87.

In the Canadian Living Test Kitchen. From left: Susan Van Hezewijk, Donna Bartolini (Test Kitchen manager), Jennifer MacKenzie, Daphna Rabinovitch (associate food director) and Elizabeth Baird (food director). Absent from photo: Heather Howe and Emily Richards.

Special Thanks

My thanks to the great team of chocolate lovers at *Canadian Living* who prepared the contents of *Canadian Living's Best Chocolate* — especially associate food director Daphna Rabinovitch, who worked with Test Kitchen home economist Emily Richards in the creation of new recipes. Happily, the recipes are seeing double service — here in the cookbook, and in the *Canadian Living* Cooking School that Daphna heads. Thanks also to the rest of the Test Kitchen staff under manager Donna Bartolini: Heather Howe, Jennifer MacKenzie and Susan Van Hezewijk, and to our valued food writers (noted on p. 90). Managing editor Susan Antonacci, senior editor Julia Armstrong, editorial assistant Olga Goncalves, plus the art department under Cate Cochran and copy department under Michael Killingsworth personify the excellence in initial preparation of the food pages for *Canadian Living*. Senior editor Beverley Renahan wears two hats in all *Canadian Living* cookbooks — first as meticulous senior editor in the magazine's food department, and secondly in an even more meticulous copy editing of the recipes for book publication. Thanks are extended to editor-in-chief Bonnie Cowan and publisher Caren King for their support in expanding *Canadian Living* beyond the pages of the magazine.

There are others to thank, too. On the visual side — our photographers (noted above), plus prop stylists Maggi Jones, Janet Walkinshaw, Shelly Tauber, Bridget Sargeant and Susan Doherty-Hannaford who provided the backgrounds, dishes and embellishments for the sets, and food stylists Kate Bush, Ruth Gangbar, Debbi Charendoff Moses, Lucie Richard, Olga Truchan, Jennifer McLagan, Jill Snider, Sharon Dale and Kathy Robertson who make the food look good enough to eat — right off the page.

Book designers Gord Sibley and Dale Vokey are responsible for the splendid design of the *Best* series.

Great appreciation goes to Madison Press Books' associate editorial director, Wanda Nowakowska, who manages to make each of the *Best* books special and unique. Help from Tina Gaudino and others at Madison Press is always appreciated. At Random House, members of the marketing and publicity departments — Kathy Bain, Pat Cairns, Sheila Kay and Cathy Paine — deserve sincere thanks, as does Duncan Shields, the indefatigable mass marketing sales manager (Ballantine Books). I appreciate the support for the *Canadian Living* cookbooks from president and publisher of Random House, David Kent, and Madison Press Books president Albert Cummings.

Elizabeth Baird

Index

Over 100 best-ever chocolate recipes — from cakes to cookies and candy.

A

Almonds
Chocolate Almond
Brittle, 84
Chocolate Almond Fruit
Strudel, 45
Chocolate Nut
Biscotti, 66
Chocolate Toffee
Squares, 75
Coffee Parfait Pie, 42
Marble Chocolate
Almond Bark, 82
Panpepato Bars, 78
Reverse Nanaimo
Bars, 78
Tarte au Chocolat, 38
White Chocolate
Carousel Cake, 13
Angel Cakes
Chocolate Espresso, 31
Apricots
and Ginger White
Chocolate Bark, 80
Chocolate Salami, 67
Chocolate Steamed
Pudding, 53
White Chocolate Apricot
Ripple Ice Cream, 61

B

Baklava
Chocolate, Nut and
Date, 46
Bananas
Bread, 50
Chocolate Banana
Cupcakes, 33
Chocolate Banana
Pudding, 54
Chocolate Fondue with
Banana Bread, 50
Chocolate Fruit, 87

Bark
Black Forest
Chocolate, 82
Fruit and Nut
Chocolate, 80
Ginger and Apricot
White Chocolate, 80
Hawaiian Plantation
Chocolate, 80
Marble Chocolate
Almond, 82
Marble Chocolate, 82
Milk Chocolate Toffee-
Pecan, 80
White Chocolate and
Cranberry, 80

BARS AND SQUARES
Brownie Ice Cream, 71
Cappuccino
Cheesecake, 75
Chocolate Pecan Pie, 77
Chocolate Toffee, 75
Cranberry Chocolate, 77
freezing, 74
Panpepato, 78
Queen of Sheba, 76
Reverse Nanaimo, 78
White Chocolate Cherry
Pecan, 74

Biscotti
Chocolate Nut, 66
Blackberries
Raspberry Blackberry
Chiffon Pie, 37
Brandy
Chocolate Bread
Pudding, 51
Chocolate Pecan
Fruitcake, 24
Chocolate Steamed
Pudding, 53
Bread Pudding
Chocolate, 51
Brittle
Chocolate Almond, 84

BROWNIES
Cheesecake Brownie
Cupcakes, 33
Chocolate Brownie
Turtle Cake, 25
Chocolate Cherry, 72
Chocolate Fudge, 72
Coffee Chocolate, 72
Cream Cheese
Raspberry, 73
Ice Cream Bars, 71
Lean but Luscious
Chocolate, 72
Nutty Chocolate, 72

Butter Tarts
Chocolate Walnut Butter
Tart Pie, 44
Buttermilk
Banana Bread, 50
Choco-Chip Buttermilk
Loaf, 30
Chocolate Banana
Cupcakes, 33
Easy Chocolate Snacking
Cake, 30
Mocha Layer Cake, 15

C

CAKES
Cappuccino Torte, 14
Choco-Chip Buttermilk
Loaf, 30
Chocolate Brownie
Turtle, 25
Chocolate Chip
Coffee, 27
Chocolate Cloud, 28
Chocolate Cookie
Cheesecake, 18
chocolate curls, 88
chocolate cutouts, 88
Chocolate Espresso
Angel, 31

Chocolate Hazelnut
Dacquoise, 8
Chocolate Indulgence, 26
Chocolate Pavlova, 20
Chocolate Peanut Butter
Mousse, 9
Chocolate Pecan
Fruitcake, 24
Chocolate Pound, 31
Chocolate Prune Rum, 28
Chocolate Pudding, 51
Chocolate Raspberry
Dome, 10
Chocolate Tiramisu
Torte, 22
Chocolate Walnut, 27
Dark Chocolate
Cheesecake, 20
Dark Chocolate Mousse
Carousel, 13
decorations, 23
Easy Chocolate
Snacking, 30
Light Chocolate Espresso
Marble Cheesecake, 18
Mocha Layer, 15
Nouvelle Bûche de
Nöel, 16
Three-Layer Chocolate
Fudge, 6
White Chocolate
Carousel, 13

CANDY. *See also* **Bark**
and **Truffles.**
Chocolate Almond
Brittle, 84
Chocolate Caramel
Popcorn Nuggets, 85
Chocolate Mice, 83
Chocolate, Fruit and Nut
Clusters, 82

Caramel
Chocolate Brownie
Turtle Cake, 25
Chocolate Caramel
Popcorn Nuggets, 85
Cheese. *See* **Cream Cheese**
and **Mascarpone.**

CHEESECAKE
Brownie Cupcakes, 33
Cappuccino Squares, 75
Chocolate Cookie, 18

Dark Chocolate, 20
Light Chocolate Espresso
Marble, 18

Cherries
Black Forest Chocolate
Bark, 82
Chocolate Bread
Pudding, 51
Chocolate Cherry
Brownies, 72
Chocolate Pecan
Fruitcake, 24
Chocolate Steamed
Pudding, 53
Chocolate, Fruit and Nut
Clusters, 82
White Chocolate Cherry
Pecan Bars, 74
Chestnuts
Chocolate Chestnut
Mousse, 53
Clementines
Chocolate Fondue, 50
Coconut
Reverse Nanaimo
Bars, 78
Coffee Cakes
Chocolate Chip, 27

COFFEE
Baked Chocolate
Mousse, 56
Cappuccino Cheesecake
Squares, 75
Cappuccino Torte, 14
Chocolate Bread
Pudding, 51
Chocolate Brownies, 72
Chocolate Espresso
Angel Cake, 31
Chocolate Indulgence
Cake, 26
Chocolate Pâté, 59
Chocolate Prune Rum
Cake, 28
Chocolate Pudding
Cake, 51
Chocolate Tiramisu
Torte, 22
Dark Chocolate
Cheesecake, 20
Double-Chocolate Drop
Cookies, 65
Easy Chocolate Snacking
Cake, 30

Fudge Truffle Tart, 38
Light Chocolate Espresso
Marble Cheesecake, 18
Light Pots de Crème, 57
Mocha Layer Cake, 15
Nouvelle Bûche de
Nöel, 16
Parfait Pie, 42

Cookie-Crumb Crusts
Chocolate Cream Pie, 42
Chocolate Cookie
Cheesecake, 18
Coffee Parfait Pie, 42
Dark Chocolate
Cheesecake, 20
Fudge Truffle Tart, 38
Light Chocolate Espresso
Marble Cheesecake, 18
Raspberry Blackberry
Chiffon Pie, 37
Very Berry Chiffon
Pie, 37

COOKIES. *See also* **BARS
AND SQUARES.**
Brutti ma Buoni, 67
Chocolate Chunk
Shortbread, 62
Chocolate Cookie
Cheesecake, 18
Chocolate Crinkle, 70
Chocolate Kisses, 65
Chocolate Nut
Biscotti, 66
Chocolate Salami, 67
Cranberry White
Chocolate Oatmeal, 64
Crunchy Chocolate
Peanut Butter
Chunks, 68
Crunchy Oatmeal
Chippers, 64
Double Chocolate
Shortbread, 62
Double Chocolate, 70
Double-Chocolate
Drop, 65
Double-Chocolate
Mint, 65
Double-Chocolate
Orange, 65
freezing, 74
Fudgy Chocolate Chip, 69
Gluten-Free Chocolate
Chip, 71

Peanut Butter Chocolate
Swirl, 68
Soft and Chewy
Chocolate Chip, 71
Soft and Chewy
Chocolate Orange, 66
White Chocolate Pecan
Rum Balls, 74

Coulis
Raspberry, 17
Cranberries
White Chocolate Bark, 80
Cranberry Chocolate
Bars, 77
Cranberry White
Chocolate Oatmeal
Cookies, 64
Fruit and Nut Chocolate
Bark, 80
Cream Cheese
and Raspberry
Brownies, 73
Cappuccino Cheesecake
Squares, 75
Cheesecake Brownie
Cupcakes, 33
Chocolate Cookie
Cheesecake, 18
Dark Chocolate
Cheesecake, 20
Light Chocolate Espresso
Marble Cheesecake, 18
Crème Brûlée
Berry Chocolate, 58
Ginger Chocolate, 58
Two-Chocolate, 58
Cupcakes
Cheesecake Brownie, 33
Chocolate Banana, 33
Curls, 88
Cutouts, 88

D

Dacquoise
Chocolate Hazelnut, 8
Dates
Chocolate Almond Fruit
Strudel, 45
Chocolate, Nut and Date
Baklava, 46

Decorations
Chocolate Garnishes, 88
Chocolate Patterns, 23
Chocolate Shell, 23

DRINKS
Chocolate Coffee
Spoons, 87
Frozen Hot Chocolate, 61
Hot Chocolate Mix, 84
Real Hot Chocolate, 84
Rich and Creamy Hot
Chocolate, 85
White Hot Chocolate, 84

F

Figs
Chocolate Almond Fruit
Strudel, 45
Fillings
Creamy, 46
Fondue
Chocolate, with Banana
Bread, 50
Fruit. *See* Apricots,
Bananas, Cherries, Dates,
Figs, Pears, Pineapples,
Raisins, Raspberries and
Strawberries.
Fudge
Chocolate Fudge
Brownies, 72
Chocolate Fudge
Sauce, 58
Chocolate Pistachio, 83
Macadamia, 82
Three-Layer Chocolate
Cake, 6

G

Garnishes, 88
Ginger
and Apricot White
Chocolate Bark, 80
Chocolate Ginger
Tassies, 45
Gluten-Free
Chocolate Chip
Cookies, 71
Grapes
Chocolate Fondue, 50

H

Hazelnuts
Brutti ma Buoni, 67
Chocolate Hazelnut
Dacquoise, 8
Chocolate Soufflé, 48
Tarte au Chocolat, 38
Truffles, 86
Honey
Chocolate, Nut and Date
Baklava, 46
Panpepato Bars, 78
Hot Chocolate, 84
Frozen, 61
Mix, 84
Rich and Creamy, 85
White, 84

I

Ice Cream
Brownie Ice Cream
Bars, 71
Chocolate, 59
Coffee Parfait Pie, 42
White Chocolate Apricot
Ripple, 61
Icing
Basic Butter, 24
Best-Ever Chocolate, 24
Chocolate Buttercream, 6

INFORMATION
Electric Mixers
Freezing Cookies, Bars
and Squares, 74
Measuring
Ingredients, 69
Melting Chocolate, 57
Storing Chocolate, 39
Toasting Pecans, 41
Types of Chocolate, 32
Walnuts, 27
Whipping Cream, 15

L

Lemon
White Chocolate Lemon
Tart, 34

Lightened Up
Crunchy Oatmeal
Chippers, 64
Double-Chocolate Drop
Cookies, 65
Double-Chocolate Mint
Cookies, 65
Double-Chocolate Orange
Cookies, 65
Easy Chocolate Snacking
Cake, 30
Lean but Luscious
Chocolate
Brownies, 72
Light Pots de Crème, 57
Loaves
Choco-Chip
Buttermilk, 30

M

Macadamia Nuts
Fudge, 82
Hawaiian Plantation
Chocolate Bark, 80
Mango
and White Chocolate
Mousse Terrine, 60
Mascarpone
Chocolate Tiramisu
Torte, 22
Nouvelle Bûche de
Nöel, 16
Strawberry White
Chocolate Tart, 41
Melting Chocolate, 57
Meringues
Chocolate Hazelnut
Dacquoise, 8
Chocolate Pavlova, 20
Chocolate Kisses, 65
Mint
Double-Chocolate Mint
Cookies, 65
Mousses
Mango and White
Chocolate Terrine, 60
Baked Chocolate, 56
Chocolate Chestnut, 53
Chocolate Mousse-Filled
Hearts, 54

N

Nanaimo Bars
Reverse, 78
Nuts. *See* Almonds,
Hazelnuts, Macadamia
Nuts, Peanuts, Pecans,
Walnuts.

O

Orange
Chocolate Cloud
Cake, 28
Chocolate Prune Rum
Cake, 28
Chocolate, Nut and Date
Baklava, 46
Double-Chocolate Orange
Cookies, 65
Light Pots de Crème, 57
Soft and Chewy
Chocolate Orange
Cookies, 66
Truffles, 86

P

Papaya
Hawaiian Plantation
Chocolate Bark, 80
Parfaits
White Chocolate and
Raspberry, 52
Pâté
Chocolate, 59
Pavlova
Chocolate, 20
Peanut Butter
Chocolate Peanut Butter
Mousse Cake, 9
Chocolate Swirl
Cookies, 68
Crunchy Chocolate
Peanut Butter
Chunks, 68
Truffles, 86
Peanuts
Chocolate, Fruit and Nut
Clusters, 82
Fruit and Nut Chocolate
Bark, 80

Pears
Chocolate Fondue, 50
Pecans
Chocolate Brownie
Turtle Cake, 25
Chocolate Chip Coffee
Cake, 27
Chocolate Pecan
Fruitcake, 24
Chocolate Pecan Pie
Squares, 77
Chocolate Pumpkin
Pie, 41
Chocolate, Nut and Date
Baklava, 46
Milk Chocolate Toffee-
Pecan Bark, 80
toasting, 41
White Chocolate Cherry
Pecan Bars, 74
White Chocolate Pecan
Rum Balls, 74
Phyllo Pastry
Chocolate Almond Fruit
Strudel, 45
Chocolate, Nut and Date
Baklava, 46
Strawberry White
Chocolate Tart, 41

PIES. *See also* **TARTS.**
Chocolate Cream, 42
Chocolate Pumpkin, 41
Chocolate Walnut Butter
Tart Pie, 44
Coffee Parfait, 42
Raspberry Blackberry
Chiffon, 37
Very Berry Chiffon, 37

Pine Nuts
Chocolate Salami, 67
Panpepato Bars, 78
Pineapple
Chocolate Pecan
Fruitcake, 24
Hawaiian Plantation
Chocolate Bark, 80
Chocolate Fondue, 50
Pistachios
Chocolate Pistachio
Fudge, 83
White Chocolate and
Cranberry Bark, 80

Plums
Lean but Luscious
Chocolate Brownies, 72
Popcorn
Chocolate Caramel
Nuggets, 85
Pots de Crème
Light, 57
Truffle, 56
Pound Cakes
Chocolate, 31
Pretzels
Chocolate-Dipped, 87
Prunes
Chocolate Prune Rum
Cake, 28
Puddings
Chocolate Banana, 54
Chocolate Bread, 51
Chocolate Pudding
Cake, 51
Chocolate Steamed, 53
Pumpkin
Chocolate Pumpkin
Pie, 41

Q

Quick Breads
Banana Bread, 50

R

Raisins
Chocolate Almond Fruit
Strudel, 45
Chocolate Pecan
Fruitcake, 24
Chocolate Salami, 67
Chocolate Steamed
Pudding, 53
Fruit and Nut Chocolate
Bark, 80
Panpepato Bars, 78
Raspberries
Chocolate Raspberry
Dome, 10
Coulis, 17
Cream Cheese Raspberry
Brownies, 73
Raspberry Blackberry
Chiffon Pie, 37
Truffles, 86

Very Berry Chiffon
Pie, 37
White Chocolate and
Raspberry Parfait, 52
Rolled Oats
Cranberry Chocolate
Bars, 77
Cranberry White
Chocolate Oatmeal
Cookies, 64
Crunchy Oatmeal
Chippers, 64
Rum
Chocolate Chestnut
Mousse, 53
Chocolate Prune Rum
Cake, 28
Nouvelle Bûche de
Nöel, 16
White Chocolate Pecan
Rum Balls, 74

S

Sauces
Chocolate Fudge, 58
Raspberry Coulis, 17
Shortbread
Chocolate Chunk, 62
Double Chocolate, 62
Soufflés
Chocolate, 48
Mini Chocolate, 48
Squares. *See* **BARS
AND SQUARES.**
Strawberries
Chocolate Fruit, 87
Chocolate Pavlova, 20
Strawberry White
Chocolate Tart, 41
Very Berry Chiffon
Pie, 37
White Chocolate
Carousel Cake, 13
Strudels
Chocolate Almond
Fruit, 45

T

TARTS
Chocolate Ginger
Tassies, 45
Chocolate Tartlets, 46
Creamy Filling, 46
Fudge Truffle, 38
Strawberry White
Chocolate, 41
Tarte au Chocolat, 38
White Chocolate
Lemon, 34

Tiramisu
Chocolate Tiramisu
Torte, 22
Toffee
Chocolate Toffee
Squares, 75
Milk Chocolate Toffee-
Pecan Bark, 80
Tortes
Cappuccino, 14
Chocolate Tiramisu, 22
Truffles
Chocolate, 86
Chocolate Caramel, 87
Chocolate Mice, 83
Hazelnut, 86
Orange, 86
Peanut Butter, 86
Raspberry, 86

W

Walnuts
Chocolate Walnut Butter
Tart Pie, 44
Chocolate Walnut
Cake, 27
Nutty Chocolate
Brownies, 72
Panpepato Bars, 78

Y

Yogurt
Raspberry Blackberry
Chiffon Pie, 37
Very Berry Chiffon
Pie, 37

Look to CANADIAN LIVING for all of the BEST!

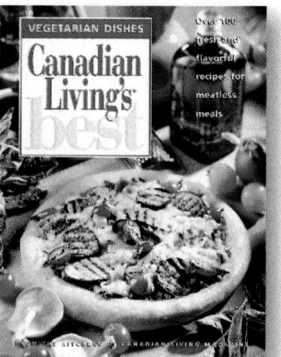

Watch for more new books in the months ahead...
from Canadian Living so you know they're —THE BEST!

CANADIAN LIVING
TESTED TILL PERFECT
KITCHEN